Calvin T

Preparing for Marriage

COUPLES' VERSION

malcolm down
PUBLISHING

Copyright © 2018 Calvin T Samuel

22 21 20 19 18   7 6 5 4 3 2 1

First published 2018 by Malcolm Down Publishing Ltd.
www.malcolmdown.co.uk

The right of Calvin T Samuel to be identified as the
author of this work has been asserted by him in accordance
with the Copyright, Designs and Patents Act 1988.

All rights reserved. No part of this publication may be reproduced,
stored in a retrieval system, or transmitted in any other form or
by any means, electronic, mechanical, photocopying, recording
or otherwise, without the prior permission of the publisher.

British Library Cataloguing in Publication Data
A catalogue record for this book is available from the British Library.

ISBN 978-1-910786-97-0 Leaders Guide
ISBN 978-1-910786-98-7 Couples Version

Unless otherwise indicated, Scripture quotations taken from
The Holy Bible, English Standard Version® (ESV®)
Copyright © 2001 by Crossway, a publishing ministry of
Good News Publishers. All rights reserved.
ESV Text Edition: 2016

The Holy Bible, English Standard Version (ESV) is adapted from
the Revised Standard Version of the Bible, copyright Division of
Christian Education of the National Council of the Churches of
Christ in the U.S.A. All rights reserved.

Some names and identifying details have been changed
to protect the privacy of individuals.

Cover design by Esther Kotecha
Art direction by Sarah Grace

Printed in the UK

CONTENTS

INTRODUCTION
Why Should We Do a Marriage Preparation Course? 5

SESSION ONE
Learn to Adjust (1) 11

SESSION TWO
Learn to Adjust (2) 21

SESSION THREE
Learn to Compromise and Forgive
(the Law of Debits and Credits) 33

SESSION FOUR
Learn to Manage Your Finances 53

SESSION FIVE
Learn to Love and Communicate 69

SESSION SIX
Learn to Express Your Sexuality 81

SESSION SEVEN
Nurturing Your Spirituality 93

INTRODUCTION

Why Should We Do a Marriage Preparation Course?

The obvious aim of a marriage prep course is to improve the quality of marriage relationships. One of the questions occasionally asked is whether there is empirical evidence that marriage preparation classes actually improve the quality of marriage relationships. Have we evidence that those who attend classes of this type are statistically less likely to face marriage breakdown than those who do not? In fact, some such research exists.

There was a research project relating to the effectiveness of a marriage course called PREP.[1] It engaged in a longitudinal study of couples over a decade, some of whom had been participants in PREP and other who were not. At the end of five years of marriage more than twice as many non-PREP couples had divorced (19 per cent) than those who had taken PREP (8 per cent). PREP couples reported lower instances of domestic violence with spouses, and greater relationship satisfaction. Importantly, the researchers compared the outcomes for PREP couples with a popular church-based marriage prep programme and observed similar outcomes.[2]

---

1. For more on this, cf. Mari Jo Renick, Susan L. Blumberg and Howard J. Markman, 'The Prevention and Relationship Enhancement Program (PREP): An Empirically Based Preventive Intervention Program for Couples', *Family Relations* Vol. 41, No. 2, April 1992, 141–147.
2, For more on this, cf. Mari Jo Renick, Susan L. Blumberg and Howard J. Markman, 141-147.

In a 2003 research paper, it was noted:

> Our findings suggest that premarital prevention programs are generally effective in producing immediate and short-term gains in interpersonal skills and overall relationship quality and that these improvements are significantly better than non-intervention couples in these areas.[3]

Preparation for marriage is important because it is acknowledged that there is greater opportunity for modification of behaviour in the earlier stages of relationship.

> Although dysfunctional communication and conflict patterns are recognizable in premarital interaction . . . they become more difficult to modify once they become established in the interactional styles of couples.[4]

In addition to formal empirical research, we can also draw upon anecdotal evidence from those who engage in marriage preparation and from those approaching a second or subsequent marriage who express regret that they were not better prepared for marriage. Marriage Care, the largest providers of marriage preparation courses in Britain, observe, 'Thousands of couples have taken some form of marriage preparation and the overwhelming feedback is that they get a lot out of it.'[5]

---

3. Jason S. Carroll and William J. Doherty, 'Evaluating the Effectiveness of Premarital Prevention Programs: A Meta-Analytic Review of Outcome Research', *Family Relations* Vol. 52, No. 2, April 2003, 105–118.
4. cf. Scott M. Stanley, Howard J. Markman, Michelle St. Peters, and B. Douglas Leber, 'Strengthening Marriages and Preventing Divorce: New Directions in Prevention Research', *Family Relations*, Vol. 44, No. 4, October 1995, 392–401.
5. http://www.marriagecare.org.uk/how-we-help/marriage-preparation/marriage-preparation-faqs/ (accessed 22 May 2017).

Given that the evidence seems to demonstrate that marriage preparation contributes to the well-being of married couples and to strengthening relationships, then marriage prep constitutes a common good.

'Relationship poverty' or 'relational poverty' might be a key term for reflection on the importance of marriage preparation. The term 'relational poverty' can be traced to Michael Schluter and David Lee's 1993 book, *The R Factor*. They argue that relationships are systematically undermined by the pressures and values of Western cultures. This is problematic precisely because relationships are key to human well-being not only in everyday life, but especially for those responsible for the deep and complex challenges of intercommunity and international relations.[6]

The term 'relationship poverty' describes not only the poverty of relationship between couples, whether already married or preparing for marriage, but also the poverty of the wider network of relationships in which couples are held and to which they in turn contribute.

To some extent a marriage prep course seeks to differentiate the marriage relationship from every other relationship. Therefore it does not simply engage with issues of relationships *and* marriage, but relationships *in* marriage, and therefore some reflection on marriage is a non-negotiable element. Marriage provides a framework around the relationship, which is more secure and stable as a result.

---

6. For more, cf. Michael Schluter and David Lee, *The R Factor*, London: Hodder & Stoughton, 1993.

EXPLORING CHRISTIAN MARRIAGE

A marriage prep course designed to prepare for Christian marriage is not a covert attempt to convert. Nonetheless, it offers an explicitly Christian perspective on marriage. Its starting point is that a request for marriage in a church building (as opposed to a registry office, beach or National Trust property) is in fact a request for Christian marriage. Such a view understands the wedding vows as a liturgical act; wedding vows are as much a promise to God as they are a means for a couple to make promises to each other.

The aim of the course, then, is first to explore the concept of Christian marriage and second, as a consequence, to explore how to build strong and resilient marriage relationships.

Such an understanding of marriage locates God not as a distant (and hopefully benevolent) figure, but as a key partner in this enterprise. Christian understandings of marriage aspire towards the ideals of divine grace (Gen. 2:18; Mk 10:6–9) and cardinal virtues such as forgiveness (Eph. 4:31–32), unconditional love (Eph. 5:28–30; Col. 3:17), and lifelong fidelity (Mal. 2:13–16; Prov. 5:15–20; 1 Cor. 7:10). Christian marriages also aspire towards integrity (Eph. 4:15; Ps. 15:2–3), mutual submission (Eph. 5:21), sexual intimacy (1 Cor. 7:3–5, Prov. 5:18–19), and transformation by divine grace (1 Cor. 7:16; 2 Cor. 3:18).

As a consequence, marriage in Christian understanding points to Christian faith not as an irrelevant or outmoded approach to life reserved for those of a religious persuasion; rather, it points to the possibility that Christian faith might be of some relevance to people's lives and to the things that are important to them.

This marriage prep course does not primarily delve into exclusively Christian content. Instead it engages with widely held ideals and concepts which are integral to marriage, such as love, trust, integrity, forgiveness, sacrifice, growth and stewardship. These concepts are not exclusively Christian, nor are they necessarily religious. However, there are explicitly Christian perspectives on each of these concepts.

This marriage prep course is designed ideally to be organised as group sessions which are intended to be a safe space within which relationships of trust can be formed, where difficult issues can be discussed and confronted, questions can be asked and explored, and the rules of engagement say something about the value of each and of all.

In more practical terms, marriage prep courses can be a wonderful place for engaged couples to network and to share ideas. Those couples much further ahead in developing wedding plans can offer advice to those who are less advanced in their planning, or simply less organised. Shared conversation about wedding planners, venues, dresses, rings, caterers, etc. become a natural part of the pre-course and post-course conversations. A number of these conversations may blossom into friendships, and a good indication of this occurs when couples start inviting other couples on the course to their wedding.

RULES OF ENGAGEMENT

A marriage prep course is not an invitation for the course leader to talk for sixty minutes. Instead, couples may be asked to read the session material ahead of a session so that it can be discussed in a meeting. The expectation is that Respect, Integrity, Courtesy and Humour (RICH) will be the hallmark of that discussion.

Speakers will not be interrupted unless it is necessary, and if so will be interrupted by the facilitator. Divergent views will not mean distempered debate.

Many couples involve at least one partner who is divorced or widowed. On the one hand, the issues that such couples explore in their relationship will not be unique. On the other hand, such couples may be more conscious than most about the challenges of marriage and will have a great deal to offer into the conversation, should they choose to do so.

CONFIDENTIALITY

Couples are encouraged to have an honest conversation. It is important to clarify expectations regarding confidentiality.

Individual partners are asked not to discuss elements of their relationship about which their partners would be unhappy. A general rule of thumb is that information which is not 'owned' should not be shared without permission.

Couples are expected to keep within the confidentiality of the group personal information which may emerge in discussion. What happens in Vegas . . .

LAUGHTER INCLUDED

Try not to be too serious. Hopefully there will be opportunity for laughter. Sometimes with others, sometimes at others. Sometimes at ourselves. If marriage prep can be fun, it bodes well for the wedding day and the marriage beyond that.

SESSION ONE

Learn to Adjust (1)

MARRIAGE IS A UNIQUE RELATIONSHIP

Christian marriage is unlike any other form of relationship. It is the only context in which we come together in the presence of our closest friends and family and make public vows in the presence of God to remain together until parted by death. Marriage demonstrates quite breath-taking ambition and requires huge commitment.

I can think of no other context and no other relationship which demands such a lifelong public commitment from us. Parenthood is perhaps the closest equivalent; one remains, of course, a parent until parted by death. But at least parents can look forward to the day when their children will move out; I know many who do! There is no similar reprieve for those who seek to keep their marriage vows. Healthy parent-child relationships tend towards greater separation and independence. Healthy marriage relationships tend towards greater togetherness and interdependence.[7]

Moreover, the lifelong intent of the marriage vows is increasingly at odds with the norms of contemporary society. Ours is a society with an increasingly short-term approach. A generation ago one might have expected to pursue a single career in a particular job or industry. The contemporary expectation is that one will have two or three careers, each potentially quite different from the others.

---

7. cf. Nicky and Sila Lee, *The Marriage Book*, London: Alpha International Publications, 2000), 17.

Our appliances and gadgets have obsolescence built in. A mobile phone is assumed to be ready for an upgrade within two years, PCs and tablets every three to four, and washing machines and refrigerators have a lifespan of around six to eight years.

No solicitor would advise a client to sign a long-term lease without the possibility of periodic reviews of the terms. Indeed, even in contexts where the language of lifetime is used, the expectation is that shorter than lifetime is envisaged. Perhaps the most debated example of this is the fact that a prison life sentence does not usually mean life. It typically means something like twenty-five years at most. With good behaviour, offenders might expect to receive parole well before this time.

The marriage vows, in contrast, do not offer any similar get-out clauses. Against the contemporary inclination to short-termism and built-in obsolescence, Christian marriage maintains its lofty ideals of permanence, of growing old together, of sharing a lifetime. The marriage vows include no possibility of parole for good behaviour, no built-in expectation of obsolescence, no renegotiation clauses, and no opportunity for periodic upgrades.

'Till death us do part' is a terrifyingly long time and a huge step into the unknown. It is the stuff of fairy tales and Hollywood romances, but very difficult to achieve in real life.

The huge ambition of the marriage vows is tempered by the reality of the divorce statistics. Increasing numbers are finding that 'till death us do part' is either too costly or simply impossible for them.[8] Nonetheless, I have yet to

---

8. ONS statistics from 2012 (the latest available) estimate that 34 per cent of marriages are expected to end in divorce by the twentieth wedding anniversary. cf. http://www.ons.gov.uk/ons/rel/vsob1/divorces-in-england-and-wales/2011/sty-what-percentage-of-marriages-end-in-divorce.html (accessed 11 January 2018).

marry any couples who did not appear to be serious about their marriage vows and who were not looking to make a serious go of them. This is especially true among couples for whom this is a second or subsequent marriage.

So how can couples improve the chances that the high ideals expressed in their marriage vows will continue to find purchase in their marriage relationship in the decades ahead? One of the key ways is by *learning to adjust.*

LEARNING TO ADJUST

One of the keys to good marriage relationships is learning to adjust. In particular, there are four areas to which couples ought to give particular attention. The first and most obvious is that of adjusting to marriage itself. Even among those who already live together, which is increasingly the norm, getting married nonetheless requires some adjustment.

Second, learning to adjust is necessary because ongoing adjustment to one another is always required. Even among couples who love one another deeply there will be personality traits or habits that you need to learn to live with over the course of a long marriage.

Third, some adjustment to roles is to be expected. Couples rarely have clearly articulated expectations of spousal roles. These roles have neither role descriptions nor regular appraisals. So how might you assess whether you are being a good spouse or whether your expectations of your spouse are within reason?

Fourth, given the lifelong ambition of the marriage vows, the only thing of which we can be certain in life is the uncertainty of life itself. Adjusting well as a couple to major life changes is an important part of maintaining healthy relationships.

ADJUSTING TO MARRIAGE

One common fallacy is that couples are always better prepared for marriage if they live together before getting married. The logic is impeccable. Those who already live together before marriage, as most do, are already exposed to their partner's less desirable traits, they are already aware of sexual compatibility issues, they go into the marriage with their eyes open, because they have effectively already had a trial run of the marriage by living together.

However, the logic is less impeccable than it appears. Simple answers to complex questions are almost always wrong. Living together may well help couples to assess whether getting married is a good idea. However, there is little evidence that those who live together before the wedding are any better prepared for marriage than their counterparts who do not.

Part of the reason for this is the argument already made that marriage is a unique form of human relationship. The exchange of public vows of lifelong commitment is unlikely to leave a relationship unchanged. At the very least, marriage raises the stakes. Living with a partner is a very significant personal commitment. However, marriage is a further step which is legally binding and brings a greater level of mutual responsibility, and indeed, expectation.

Living with a boyfriend who has personality traits you find problematic is one thing. To make public vows to spend the rest of your life with him for better or worse is another thing entirely. It is this which requires adjustment even among couples already living together by the time of their marriage.

A husband is not quite the same animal as a live-in boyfriend, nor is a wife quite the same as a live-in girlfriend.

Even when there are children, a marriage changes the relationship. This is not only true psychologically because of the raised stakes, it is also true in some mystical way that is difficult to articulate and even more difficult to quantify.

Some Christians describe the marriage bond as a spiritual reality, others as a sacramental one. Many who would not naturally use that type of language nonetheless see something sacred and mystical about the marriage relationship. Christian marriage is far more than a legal document formalising a pre-existing relationship. It is a pledge towards a different kind of relationship which is not self-seeking and is rooted in a public commitment to the other 'for better for worse, for richer for poorer, in sickness and in health ... till death us do part'.[9]

What living together can never do, whether before or after a marriage, is magically enable couples to become less self-centred or more forgiving, both of which are crucial areas of adjustments to be made for successful relationships.

> Tom remembers well the early days of his marriage. He married his long-time friend, whom he had first met at sixteen. They had been through a whole range of experiences as part of a wider peer group and formed a deep and trusting friendship. However, it was not until nearly a decade after they had first met that he realised that their friendship had become something more, and within eighteen months had asked her to marry him. She said yes ...
>
> When they married six months later, Tom was wonderfully happy – but by the time of

---

9. cf. Book of Common Prayer.

the honeymoon, he was discontent. It was very difficult to put his finger on the source of his discontentment. Tom was not the only one. His new wife felt similar discontent.

Together they saw their marriage prep counsellor who helped them put their finger on the issue. She offered a single word: Adjustment. They were struggling to adjust to one another, to the roles of husband and wife, to their different rhythms and personalities, to the realities of married life.

Many married couples report similar feelings. There is often tremendous guilt associated with those feelings, not least when it is a long-term relationship. Couples wonder whether they have made a terrible mistake or whether the shackles of marriage have killed the free spirit of their love. For those whose previous marriage ended in divorce or by becoming widowed, such feelings can sometimes be even more acute, because of a fear of repeating past mistakes. In most cases, these fears are unfounded.

The feelings of discontent are often to do with the process of adjustment to a new situation. If couples can simply recognise that their feelings are not necessarily long-term, nor are they directed primarily at their spouse but at their own feelings of unsettledness at a new situation, then they might avoid saying or doing things which can make a tricky situation worse.

ADJUSTING TO ONE ANOTHER

Adjustment to the very fact of being married is made a little more complex because it is clear that very few couples are married to their ideal partner, for the simple reason that the ideal partner does not exist.

Our spouses are wonderful and gifted people, full of life and love, and a unique combination of things that we adore and other elements we might prefer were not present. Nonetheless, they are created in the image of God and constitute a divine gift which enriches not only our lives but also the lives of many others besides.

What they are not, is perfect. What is more, even if they were perfect we would still find something objectionable in them, precisely because we are not perfect, and their perfection would bring into sharp focus our own imperfections.

Most couples who have been together for some time recognise that the object of their affection, though wonderful, has certain qualities, habits or attitudes which each finds unattractive. Many, if they had the option, would prefer that those objectionable elements were overcome or removed. Some enter the relationship with the unspoken intent of gradually 'improving' their partners, whilst others simply have blind optimism that their partner will outgrow their less attractive qualities.

Most couples at some point come to the realisation that their partner is not going to change, because those qualities that one finds objectionable are part of who they are. They are no more likely to change that aspect of who they are than they are to change eye colour.

For those who are perfectionists, in particular, this is a difficult truth, and a significant challenge. Will you love your partner as they are, warts and all, or will you choose instead to love the person you hope or imagine they might one day become?

The latter choice is the easier one. The more challenging, and indeed more Christian choice, is to love the person before you today. In order to do this with integrity, some adjustment of expectations is required.

Many couples adjust to one another as a natural consequence of being part of a loving relationship.

> Dan and Amy are Newcastle United season ticket holders. Dan grew up as a Newcastle United supporter, his dad was a Newcastle supporter, and his dad before him, and presumably his dad before him as well. Amy married into the team, as it were, already a football fan, but adopted the team loyalties at some point early in the relationship. Whether the rumours are true that there was a prenuptial agreement requiring support for Newcastle United, or indeed whether it was an immediate or gradual adoption, is not clear. What is clear is that Newcastle is now very much their team.

However, it is also true that many couples struggle to adjust to their differences in personality, or indeed see little reason to adjust.

> Sam and Monica have very different personality types. In Myers-Briggs terms, Monica is INTJ (Introvert, iNntuitive, Thinking, Judging) and Sam is ENFP (Extrovert, iNtuitive, Feeling, Perceiving). They are therefore almost the exact opposite personality types.
>
> This means that if Sam likes something, Monica is unlikely to, and vice versa. What she thinks is a stimulating way to spend an afternoon he finds boring or, worse, frustrating. Her approach

to life often seems unadventurous to a man who loves spontaneity. Sam's approach to life is incomprehensible to a woman who loves order and predictability.

Not only do they continue to have difficulty adjusting to one another, even after many years of marriage, neither really wants to adjust to a way of being that is at odds with their basic personality. Monica doesn't really want to be become a spontaneous person, and would have no idea how to become one even if she wanted to. Neither does Sam want to become a bore who feels the need to plan insignificant details of life. Nonetheless, they are committed to one another and to the marriage and continue to learn how to adjust to one another.

Opposites do certainly attract; they nonetheless often find it a challenge to live together in harmony. Attraction happens in a moment. Living in harmony is the work of a lifetime.

DISCUSSION

1. What are your reflections so far on learning to adjust?
2. What are the areas in marriage that you can already identify as potentially difficult points of adjustment?
3. How have you already navigated some of the challenges of adjustment outlined in today's session?

A CONCLUDING PRAYER

This or some other prayer:

Creator God, who brings light out of darkness and order out of chaos,
the author of peace and lover of concord,
who knows us better than we know ourselves,
draw us to yourself and transform us by your grace.
May all who seek to grow in love,
to love another as themselves,
encounter the God who is Love.
Amen.

SESSION TWO

Learn to Adjust (2)

ADJUSTING TO ROLES

People have a range of expectations and assumptions about the roles of an ideal husband or wife. Very rarely are these subject to critical reflection and even more rarely are they openly owned and discussed. The inevitable consequence is that expectations will not be met and disappointment is the likely result.

Often men describe the ideal husband in functional terms. An ideal husband protects, provides, and is caring, organised, loving, gentle and faithful. He is strong, considerate and reliable. In contrast, women often describe an ideal husband in relational terms. An ideal husband is supportive, encouraging, humorous and loyal. He knows how to have fun, is a good friend, brilliant with children, sexy and good at making decisions.

Obviously there are areas of overlap in these lists, but the potential for discontent is obvious if a husband thinks his primary role is to protect, provide and organise whilst his wife thinks his primary role is to be supportive, encouraging and humorous. #EpicFail is only a matter of time.

Newlyweds, regardless of how long they have been a couple, or whether they already live together or not, will need to adjust to their new roles of husband and wife. Even more crucially, they will also need to adjust both their expectations of their own role and that of their spouse.

We draw our ideas of the ideal husband and wife from a wide range of sources. Some are surprising, most a little irrational, but they are nonetheless often deep-seated and subconscious. It's easy, for example, to assume that a good husband looks a bit like our own father (if relationships are warm) or is everything he is not (if relationships are difficult).

If such deep-seated and often subconscious expectations of spousal roles are to undergo any form of adjustment, it will not be the result of simply hoping for the best. They need to be owned and discussed openly.

This is especially true for those who have been divorced or widowed, and whose understanding of an ideal husband or wife is likely to have been shaped, for good or ill, by their previous experience of marriage. It is important to find ways of talking through those assumptions and acknowledging the impact of that history.

Some of these expectations are largely harmless.

> James: My wife, who likes to think of herself as an independent woman, nonetheless does not think that changing light bulbs might in any way be her responsibility. If there is a blown light bulb somewhere in the house, which I appear not to have noticed, she may casually drop into the conversation the fact that there appears to be a blown light bulb in the dining room.
>
> In over twenty years of marriage she has never, in my recollection, asked me to change a light bulb, nor has she ever, to my knowledge, changed one herself. She has simply assumed that this is part of my role as the man of the house. I have long suspected that if by some freak of nature all the light bulbs in the house were blown, she'd sit

quietly in the dark until I got home, whereupon she'd point out gently that I had a light bulb problem.

I have no idea where or why she got this idea, or how long she has held it. It is simply there. The reality is that I have adjusted to this role. When we first married I certainly didn't think that my role as a husband included being Head of the Department for Light Bulbs. But I do now...

Some expectations can be more problematic:

> Edith: One of my husband's subconscious views of an ideal wife is that she should be Head of Catering. He knows it sounds terribly old-fashioned and misogynistic, but his ideal wife cooks for her family.
>
> I trace this back to his mum, who was always clear that household chores were not her responsibility. Rather, they were the responsibility of her children. So when they washed dishes, cleaned the bathroom, swept the floor, did laundry or washed the windows, they weren't doing their mum a favour. No, they were doing *their chores.*
>
> The single role that was unequivocally Mum's responsibility was cooking. It was not the case that none of the children did any cooking. They did. Frequently. But when they did so, it was with the understanding that they were lending a helping hand in *Mother's role.*
>
> As a consequence he is very happy to do most household chores without complaint. Point him at dirty dishes, vacuuming, ironing, laundry or a bathroom in need of urgent attention and he has

little resistance to doing those household tasks, though it's probably best to keep him away from laundering whites. Bad things can happen... But there is an unspoken (and frankly unreasonable) expectation that his wife should do the cooking.

When we first married, this was a source of great tension. Because we had not discussed expectation of roles, I initially was pleased that my new husband appeared to be a 'new' man, happy to do his fair share of household chores. Not unreasonably, I assumed that this meant that he would be open to sharing responsibility for cooking. He was not...

Even worse, he had not articulated that he was not; and he certainly could not coherently articulate why he was happy to clean but not to cook. Partly, this was because it was a subconscious expectation of his role as a husband and my role as a wife. Partly it was because we were both taken by surprise how deeply in his psyche his particular assumptions about the role of a wife and mother were rooted.

Once couples are able to identify and articulate expectations of spousal roles they can begin to have constructive conversations. Even more importantly, they can begin to adjust expectations.

How might conflicting role expectations be resolved?

There is no magic bullet or quick fix to conflicting role expectations. However, there are steps that can be taken. Here are five steps to take in seeking to adjust to role expectations.

1. Be honest about your expectations

Even if your expectations about the relative roles of a husband and wife are irrational, they are there. It is best to be honest about them, even if you are embarrassed about them. If your expectation of an ideal spouse is that they bring you slippers and a newspaper/magazine as soon as you enter the house, be honest about it. (And prepare for disappointment and derision.)

2. Don't begin anything that you are not prepared to continue

The classic rookie mistake for newlyweds is to begin their marriage behaving in ways that they have no intention of sustaining, or which are simply not sustainable. If you begin your married life by taking your spouse breakfast in bed every Sunday morning followed by a relaxing massage (assuming they like that sort of thing), your spouse is quite likely to begin to see this as your normal way of demonstrating affection.

When you get bored with this or decide that this was an introductory offer only, don't be surprised if your spouse speculates whether you might be changing your mind about the marriage itself.

3. Consider how far you can adjust with integrity

Having talked with your spouse about role expectations, each needs to consider how far they can move on from their own starting point. This is the moment of adjustment.

Hearing your wife articulate what she thinks an ideal husband might be may be an inspiration. Alternatively, it might simply reinforce insecurities and undermine self-esteem. Couples will need to consider how they can adjust without losing something of their integrity. We bring who we are to a marriage. We do not simply capitulate to whatever our spouse's perceptions may be of the ideal.

4. Feel free to disagree gently

An honest discussion of spousal roles will almost inevitably lead to disagreement. Both parties are unlikely to be reading from the same script. Feel free to disagree. Gently. The disagreement will hopefully lead to some compromise agreement at a later stage. But it might be *much* later. Explore win-win resolutions rather than win-lose.

5. Keep working at it

Adjustment to roles is not merely of relevance to newlyweds. Spousal roles continue to change over time because the family continues to develop and grow and mature. It is a fallacy that you can sort our spousal roles at the beginning and then sail smoothly into the future, because the future is uncertain. The roles will need revising at numerous points in the course of the marriage.

ADJUSTING TO LIFE

Just about the only thing in life that is certain is that life is uncertain. The wedding vows capture some of that expectation of uncertainty. 'For better for worse, for richer for poorer, in sickness and in health' gives some insight into the range of possibilities.

There are many other elements of married life that might have been included in the marriage vows, but which are merely hinted at in the phrase 'for better, for worse'. My suggestions would include: in childbirth and childrearing, in sleepless nights and nappy changes, through parents' evenings and teenage tantrums, career changes and redundancies, bereavements and house moves, betrayals or personal tragedy.

To take the marriage vows seriously is to seek to journey through life with an additional certainty beyond the uncertainty of life. It is the certainty of having a spouse who is committed to standing beside you whatever life throws at you.

Successful couples not only need to learn to adjust to marriage, to one another, to their expectations of spousal roles, but also to life itself. Pressures of everyday life put a strain on relationships, and it is those couples that learn to adjust who survive and flourish.

Every marriage relationship faces its own challenges from within, supplemented by challenges from without. Each year marriages run aground on the submerged sandbanks of demanding careers or personal tragedy, overbearing in-laws and financial struggles, or the demands of parenting.

The capacity to adjust course in order to respond appropriately to external conditions is quite often what differentiates successful marriages from those that run aground.

The contemporary family faces multiple pressures. It is increasingly the norm for both adults to be in employment and indeed to change employment several times. Finding a rhythm of married life that is nurturing of the family, offering opportunities to grow together and to flourish, is a critical part of human well-being.

The importance of rhythm should not be underestimated. Creatures of habit particularly appreciate regular rhythms which enable them, like the needle of an old-fashioned record player, to find a groove which releases a soothing or stimulating harmony. When the needle skips out of that groove, discord is the inevitable and predictable result, and the likelihood of doing permanent damage is very high.

Rhythm, the regular repeated patterns of movement or sound, is important in managing levels of stress, particularly when internalised. If you have had the opportunity to observe a learner driver, or indeed to teach someone to drive, you notice how hard they have to concentrate in order to process the stream of sensory information and feedback that is a necessary part of driving on public roads.

Other motorists, Highway Code restrictions, passengers, cyclists and maintaining appropriate levels of hazard awareness require a great deal of attention. At precisely the same time, the learner driver is trying to modulate the clutch, brake and accelerator pedals with their feet, keeping the vehicle on track with their hands, and watching no fewer than three different rear-view mirrors without losing track of what is going on ahead and around them, whilst maintaining a speed appropriate to the prevailing conditions.

When described in this way, it is a miracle that anyone can drive at all! Learner drivers initially struggle to figure out how it can be done, and we may have seen them wide-eyed on quiet roads trying to figure it out, occasionally accompanied by wild-eyed driving instructors.

Eventually, learner drivers must find a rhythm which enables them instinctively to modulate pedals and manage steering inputs, which leaves their brain freer to pay attention to what is going on around them. The result is an immediate and dramatic fall in the amount of energy it takes simply to keep the car on the road, because they have found a rhythm.

If they fail to find that rhythm, they are unlikely ever to pass a driving test and even if they did, driving would be so mentally and emotionally exhausting they would be unlikely to do it willingly.

After many years, some experienced drivers are able to drive so instinctively that it is possible to travel along a familiar stretch of road with virtually no recollection of the journey because the journey is part of a regular rhythm.

This is what adjusting to life looks and feels like. When we are yet to find a rhythm, we are learner drivers overloaded with sensory information which is unfamiliar and uncomfortable. We make mistakes and carry a great deal of stress. And we pass on our stress to everyone who is on the journey with us.

Once we have learned to adjust, when we have found a sustainable rhythm, we have the spare capacity to concentrate on other things, and the stress levels of everyone sharing the journey falls.

Unlike driving, life is not a skill to be learned once. Family life repeatedly faces upheaval, sometimes for very positive reasons, such as a new job, a new home or a new baby, sometimes for less positive reasons, such as bereavement or major illness.

> Rosie: I remember well September 2001. I started a new job after twelve months on maternity leave. Our daughter started primary school and our one-year-old was starting at a child minder's. And my husband? He was starting part-time study alongside full-time employment. It was a very difficult time as a family. It was a difficult time for the marriage. There was a great deal of adjusting to do before we found a new rhythm which made sense of our changed circumstances. The challenge was not to do too much damage to the relationship whilst the needle was trying to find a new groove.

Nearly fourteen years later, we are again experiencing similar upheaval. I am again taking on a new job, my husband is also starting a new job, our daughter is at the beginning of her A level course and our son is beginning his GCSE course. We can already anticipate the difficulty in finding a new rhythm, even though we cannot predict the ways in which that new rhythm might develop.

DISCUSSION

1. What are your reflections on sessions 1 and 2 of Learn to Adjust?

2. Did you learn anything about your partner that you did not already know? If so, what?

3. How long do you find that it takes you to adjust to a new situation?

4. How have you already navigated some of the challenges of adjustment outlined in this session?

5. Continue in conversation about some of the issues raised around learning to adjust after you leave. If you have not yet had an open conversation about your expectations of spouse roles, this is a great time to do so.

A CONCLUDING PRAYER

This or some other prayer:

Loving God, who sees us as we are and loves us still, who knows our faults, failings and broken relationships

and loves us still,
who has created all things bright and beautiful . . .
. . . yet loves us still;
teach us to love and be loved by each other,
forgive us for impatience and ill temper,
and free us from our sinfulness
that we might become all that you have created us to be.
Amen.

SESSION THREE

Learn to Compromise and Forgive (The Law of Debits and Credits)

CONFLICT, FORGIVENESS, COMPROMISE AND INVESTMENT

All relationships will at some point face conflict. Conflict is at heart about disagreement or difference of viewpoint or opinion. Conflict is a potentially creative or destructive tension, and is inevitable when different personalities and people are placed into close proximity on a shared project. There are few greater 'shared projects' than a marriage.

The sources of conflict are complex. Many conflicts are more apparent than real, the result of misunderstanding or a clash of personalities. More substantial conflicts are the consequence of disagreements about process, objectives, roles or ideology. The most complex and intractable conflicts are a destructive combination of misunderstanding, disagreement, distrust and defensiveness.

Some situations of conflict are minor and inconsequential: which television programme shall we watch tonight? Others are more significant and ideological: what value systems do we want to pass on to our children? Some conflict is the result of triangulation, where conflict is displaced from another context into the marriage relationship. For example, a husband has a hard day at work but displaces the conflict by taking it out on his wife and family.

All conflict has the potential to be destructive, particularly when it is protracted and personalised. Nonetheless, conflict is not necessarily negative. Indeed, conflict can lead to creative spaces in which, combined with honesty and vulnerability, the conflict may lead to a positive outcome.

Conflict is an invitation to see the world through the eyes of another. When handled positively, conflict can be a means through which issues can be clarified or reassessed, and greater honesty about delicate issues may be owned and expressed. Indeed, conflict resolution can lead to deepening the relationship. Conflict, when resolved well, is a muscle that strengthens relationships as deeply as intimacy.

Negatively, however, unresolved conflict can lead to bitterness and a deepening of differences, real or perceived. It is most difficult when conflict results in personal attacks rather than disagreement around a set of issues.

Conflict is an inevitable and necessary part of all marriage relationships. Couples often find themselves in conflict around the same five issues: money, sex, work, parenting and housework.[10] Conflict is the other side of the coin of learning to adjust. So, how might couples learn how to handle conflict positively rather than negatively?

INVESTING IN RELATIONSHIP: THE LAW OF DEBITS AND CREDITS

Strong relationships require investment of time, energy and emotion. They require selflessness, giving up and giving in, loving another as oneself. That investment is necessary in order to build up the levels of trust and goodwill, which enable relationships to function and ultimately to flourish.

---

10. Read more at http://www.relevantmagazine.com/life/relationships/5-biggest-areas-conflict-couples#3rXV5ZLthlp9ebGq.99 (accessed 20 December 2017).

Like all relationships, a marriage requires ongoing investment. Moreover, because a marriage is an intimate relationship of love, trust, commitment and mutual self-giving, it requires a lifetime of investment of time, energy and emotion.

Relationship breakdown is rarely the result of a failure of love. Rather, it is more commonly the result of a failure of trust, or forgiveness, a failure to find common ground or creative resolution to conflict.

> Rosner, whose parents were divorced but remained close friends, described them as two people whose relationship had been improved by their divorce. They clearly cared about each another and could figure out how to be good friends but had made each other miserable whilst married. At some point, their marriage had floundered into bankruptcy. Despite the fact that they cared for one another, the relationship broke down.

Conversely, there are marriage relationships that survive betrayal, where one or both spouses have been unfaithful. In some of these cases, the marriage has not merely survived but has gone on to thrive after hitting a catastrophic low point. In these instances couples have found ways, no doubt painful and costly, of moving beyond a period of deep hurt and betrayal into a new future of trust and mutual forgiveness.

How is it that some relationships find ways to navigate through the stormy waters of betrayal, hurt and conflict and manage to survive deep trauma, whilst others run aground? I suggest is it is primarily to do with the Law of Debits and Credits.

EXPLORING THE LAW OF DEBITS AND CREDITS

One helpful way of thinking of relationships is to imagine that they are not unlike bank accounts in which we build up and store capital that we will need to draw upon at some later stage. Some people manage their accounts well, keeping it in credit so that there is always something to draw upon when they need it. Others are less attentive to managing their accounts so they find themselves occasionally overdrawn, trying to draw on capital that they have already spent. They find themselves in the embarrassing situation of having their withdrawal declined or cheques bounced.

The big difference between bank accounts and relationships is that most bank accounts provide us with regular statements, which allow us to check our balances. We are inundated with ways of doing this. In addition to the traditional regular printed bank statements, we can get updates from cash machines or make use of telephone banking, internet banking, and apps on our smart devices.

A recent advert from my bank included an invitation to download their app to my 'smart watch' so that I would never be too far away from my bank balances! A number of banks also offer balance warnings so that we receive a text informing us when our balance has fallen below a certain level.

In sharp contrast, we never receive monthly statements about the balance of our relationships. There is no easy way to log on to ensure that our relationships aren't overdrawn or heading for bankruptcy. There is no app to warn us when we are headed into dangerously low credit. The only way we can discover the level of our relationship credit is to ask our spouse.

Building up 'relationship credit' is important for healthy relationships because each of us will need to draw upon that goodwill at some point when we disappoint, hurt or fall out with our spouse. We will need to draw upon that goodwill when we are seeking creative solutions to conflict, or perhaps rebuilding trust after damaging conflict.

What is it that enables some relationships to survive a big hit of betrayal, hurt or disappointment, and to navigate successfully through conflict? I suggest that these are relationships with a great deal of credit in them, able to afford large withdrawals. To shift metaphors a little, these are relationships which have previously earned a great deal of brownie points and are therefore more likely to be able to recover after hurt, disappointment or betrayal than those which were running low on brownie points to begin with. For brownie points, feel free to substitute Nectar points or Clubcard points if you prefer. The analogy holds.

One of the fascinating things about human behaviour is our inclination to interpret events in light of previously held convictions. So if you are in a relationship with someone whom you are fully persuaded is kind, loving and considerate, but who then behaves in a way that is not kind or loving or considerate, you are inclined to ask whether there is something wrong with your loved one because in your estimation, for them to behave in that way is *out of character*.

However, if someone else about whom you hold a far lower opinion – someone you already think to be rude and inconsiderate – were to exhibit virtually identical behaviour, you would be less likely to rationalise their behaviour because it is consistent with your previously held conviction. In this latter case, you don't enquire what may be wrong. Instead, their misbehaviour reinforces your prior convictions. In your estimation, this behaviour is very much part of *their character.*

Similarly, if my opinion of someone is that they are always late, when they are late (again) I roll my eyes (politely) and think to myself that they really need to get their act together. They receive little sympathy. However, if someone whom I think of as a real stickler for time happens to run late on one occasion, I am far more likely to overlook this misdemeanour. Their lateness on this occasion does not define them in my estimation.

In each example, reaction to the misdemeanour is based not so much on what a person has done as much as it is upon the quality of the existing relationship, and prior perceptions of that person. Put another way, people who are late or inconsiderate either draw upon goodwill that they have already built up, or discover that they have no goodwill built up upon which they can draw.

If it is true that relationships work based upon goodwill and trust (and brownie or Nectar points), then the obvious question is: how do you go about intentionally building up relationship credit, knowing that at some point we all make withdrawals from our bank of goodwill?

Indeed, most people make tiny withdrawals from their relationship accounts every day by small slights, irritations and disappointments. In addition, most married couples use up a large number of brownie points because of some significant failing at various points in a marriage. These withdrawals are not usually intentional or premeditated, though sometimes they are. Rather, they are the inevitable consequence of human imperfection and selfishness. They result from mishandled conflict, miscommunication and misunderstanding as much as from misbehaviour.

So the key question is: how do we build strong relationships with enough credit, enough brownie points, within them to be able to withstand the debits that will inevitably come our way? I suggest that the two most effective ways of building up relationship credits is via the Way of Forgiveness and the Path of Compromise.

THE WAY OF FORGIVENESS

Forgiveness is a cardinal Christian virtue. Jesus taught his disciples to pray: 'Forgive us our sins, for we ourselves forgive everyone indebted to us' (Luke 11:4).

When Peter asked Jesus whether he should forgive as much as seven times each day for the same offence, Jesus' reply was outrageous. Not seven times but 'seventy times seven' (Matt. 18:22). Each day!

Jesus embodies and models extravagant forgiveness when he prays for those in the act of nailing him to the cross: 'Father, forgive them, for they know not what they do' (Luke 23:34). Significantly, Jesus' last act in Luke's Gospel before his death is an offer of forgiveness to the dying thief: 'Today you will be with me in Paradise' (Luke 23:43).

Desmond Tutu's book, *No Future Without Forgiveness*, charts the work of South Africa's Truth and Reconciliation Commission, which he chaired in the aftermath of apartheid.[11] He argues persuasively that it was the quality of forgiveness that preserved South Africa from descending into civil war after the fall of the brutal apartheid regime. Forgiveness was a major factor in seeking creative resolution to South African conflict.

---

11. Desmond Tutu, *No Future Without Forgiveness*, London: Rider, 2000.

Forgiveness is not based on justice or fair play; rather, it is based paradoxically on love and self-interest. When we seek forgiveness it is not because we deserve to be forgiven, but precisely because we do not. However, when we forgive, the person who benefits most from our forgiveness is not the wrongdoer but rather the wronged, especially in cases when wrongdoers are unrepentant. When faced with someone who loses no sleep because they have wronged us, the best thing that we can do is to forgive, not primarily for their benefit but our own.

This is unconditional forgiveness, which is to recognise that the wrong that has been done to us can never be undone and even if we were to take our revenge, which might make us feel better for a while, it still can neither repay the debt, nor undo the damage. In such a case, the only thing that we can do that is constructive and healing, both for ourselves and for those who have wronged us, is to forgive. However, forgiveness is always costly.

Lest we think that such unconditional forgiveness is anything other than excruciatingly difficult, we might recall Anglican priest Julie Nicholson, who resigned from her parish in 2006 because at that point she could not forgive those who had taken her daughter's life in the 7/7 London Underground bombings. In her case, those who had taken her daughter's life had also taken their own. Forgiveness is not based on justice, but rather on love and self-interest.

But forgiveness is not primarily based on self-interest; it is primarily rooted in love, which expresses itself most powerfully in care for the other. We might describe forgiveness offered in response to repentance and request as conditional forgiveness, as opposed to unconditional forgiveness, which is offered even when it is both undesired and undeserved.

Forgiveness offered in response to repentance and request leads to renewed relationship. 'Today you will be *with me* in Paradise' is Jesus' response to the thief who asked for forgiveness.[12]

Those in marriage relationships need both to offer and to receive forgiveness, firstly because we are in need of it. However, secondly, that forgiveness has the effect of deepening relationships is a happy coincidence. Why does forgiveness deepen relationships? Why should it build up relationship credits? There are three primary reasons.

First, forgiveness is about cancelling debts. It is at heart a financial term.

> Years ago when I worked in the loans department of a bank, the bank made a financial decision not to pursue a number of its worst debtors, simply because it would cost the bank more to recover the debts than the value of the debts themselves. So the debts were cancelled and the technical term used was that the debts were *forgiven*. That which had previously come between the two parties had been removed, deleted, cancelled.

Forgiveness, when freely offered and received, inevitably deepens relationship by the simple expedient of removing that which gets in the way of closer fellowship.

Second, forgiveness is always undeserved; otherwise it is not forgiveness. Those who genuinely seek forgiveness recognise that they cannot argue for extenuating circumstances. If there were extenuating circumstances then it is not forgiveness that they seek but exoneration.

---

12. Emphasis mine.

Similarly, they recognise that they cannot offer excuses or seek to defend themselves or their actions. To do so is not to seek forgiveness but rather to seek justification.

Those who genuinely seek forgiveness know that they are in the wrong. Forgiveness cannot be argued for, nor is it the result of a skilful defence.

Forgiveness deepens relationships because those who are forgiven know that the one who forgives them has chosen the way of forgiveness rather than retaliation. They are painfully aware that their debts, which cannot be repaid, have been cancelled.

Third, forgiveness is principally an act of love. Love begets love, as surely as hatred begets hatred.

Those who receive forgiveness, aware that it is undeserved, and conscious of the high cost of following the path of forgiveness rather than retaliation, love more deeply in response. Jesus observes in Luke 7:47 that the one who is forgiven little loves little, but the one whose many sins are forgiven shows great love.

Those seeking to credit their relationship account, desiring to build up strong relationships which can withstand the big debits and withdrawals that inevitably come, must learn to forgive.

However, this is easier said than done. Forgiveness is not a natural response to being wronged, even when we love those who wrong us. Indeed, it is often more difficult to forgive loved ones who wrong us because we hold higher expectations of them. Learning to forgive those we love is a lifetime occupation.

THE PATH OF COMPROMISE

If forgiveness is a cardinal Christian virtue, and a gospel principle we see embodied and modelled most clearly in Jesus, compromise is the prerequisite value for successful relationships.

Compromise is the next step on from learning to adjust and presumes a situation of conflict to which it seeks to offer a creative solution.

The best forms of compromise pursue a win-win outcome rather than a win-lose outcome. Conversely, the worst attempts at compromise result in a lose-lose outcome, i.e. a solution which is satisfactory to neither party. King Solomon (1 Kings 3:16–28) famously proposed a lose-lose compromise between two mothers who argued over a baby, by suggesting he would divide the child in half!

A win-win approach to compromise does not suggest that each attempt at compromise will result in a win for both parties. Rather, a win-win approach is to take an overarching view which means that each party will win on some issues and lose on others so that overall both parties feel that the issues which matter to them have been taken into consideration.

On some issues it is extremely difficult to achieve compromise, either because they matter deeply or perhaps because the issues are viewed as representative of more significant interests which we are seeking to defend.

On other issues it is comparatively easy to find compromise. These issues do not matter deeply to us; they fall into the category of preference rather than non-negotiable. Nonetheless, it would be a mistake to think that compromise is anything other than hard work in a relationship.

Grace: Both my husband and I really enjoy watching films. However, we tend not like the same kinds of films. He likes action films; explosions, high-speed car chases, hand-to-hand combat, high adrenaline, and did I mention explosions? I like rom-coms and chick-flicks; the combination of romance and laughter is hard to beat. My films are typically not his cup of tea, nor are his films mine. Unless they involve Will Smith... Then we are on common ground!

In the early days of our marriage, in the days before you could simply check online to see what was on at the local cinema, this was a source of real tension in the relationship. We would get to the cinema and try to decide what to watch once we were there. Obviously, he didn't want to watch a chick-flick and I didn't want to watch another boys-with-toys film. So there were occasions when we returned home from the cinema not having watched a film because we could not agree on which film to watch!

In later years we learned to compromise. Compromise for us was not to watch a film that neither of us was interested in. Rather, it was for him to watch the occasional rom-com whilst I watched the occasional action movie.

We have worked on compromise over the years and two things have emerged. First, he has learnt to enjoy (discreetly) the odd chick-flick and I have discovered an appreciation for some action films. Second, and far more important, we have both discovered how significantly compromise can add to our relationship credits.

> I recognise that my husband would probably rather have his hair braided and eyebrows plucked than go to the cinema to watch a chick-flick. That he is occasionally prepared to do so says something about the way he feels about me and values our relationship.
>
> Similarly, he recognises that I would probably prefer to go to the dentist than to watch some of his films! Still, I have dutifully accompanied him to watch films in which I have no interest. If he were in any doubt about this, the fact that I have been known to fall asleep in the cinema despite the loud explosions indicates the level of boredom . . . That I am prepared occasionally to do this speaks volumes about the way I feel about him and the value I place on our relationship.

Because couples know each other, they recognise the compromise that the other is prepared to make and value it appropriately. Moreover, these small gestures make us predisposed to responding in kind. As I said above, love begets love.

Most compromises are far more significant than deciding which film to watch, and are usually far more costly. However, such compromises also have the capacity to elicit a far more deep-seated response in kind.

> Many years ago, Sam had the chance to study at the university he had dreamed of attending as a child. It was genuinely a once-in-a-lifetime opportunity. There was a catch, however. In fact, there were two. First, it was horrendously expensive and he and his wife didn't have the means to afford it.

Second, it would also have meant moving and therefore would have required his wife, Monica, to give up her job.

However, when Sam shared this exciting possibility with Monica, she was entirely unfazed. She was happy to give up her job and to join him in plunging into debt in order to pursue his dream.

As life worked out, they were unfortunately simply unable to raise the money to pursue that dream and so Sam was not able to take up the place. This meant that Monica was not put in the position of being asked to give up her job to pursue his dreams. However, even though she hadn't been placed in that position, Sam valued deeply her unhesitating willingness to give up what she was doing in order to support him because she knew how much it meant to him. Monica had no idea, and it certainly was not her primary aim, but in being willing to support her husband in this way, she was making a huge deposit into her relationship credit.

Some years later, an opportunity came up for Monica to pursue her dream to study performing arts. It was a tricky time with two young children to manage. However, Sam didn't hesitate to support her in this, in part because it was a good thing for her, but also in part because he had not forgotten that this was the woman who had been prepared to put her plans on hold to support *his* dream. Monica had no idea, but she was at this point harvesting goodwill she had sown many years previously. Indeed, it was only as Monica heard Sam tell the story to others that she realised how deeply her selflessness had impacted upon her husband. She had been acting naturally, out of love.

Compromise requires giving up and giving in; it is an act of selflessness, where we seek the well-being of the other rather than ourselves. Selflessness is not without risk. We fear being taken advantage of, that our spouses may repeatedly allow us to be selfless. We fear that if we act selflessly our selflessness may not be reciprocated.

This is neither an unreasonable nor unfounded fear. If one's spouse is self-centred and narcissistic, it is entirely possible that they might respond to selflessness with selfishness. Alternatively, the memories of a previous relationship where similar self-centred behaviour was exhibited might cause fear even if one's spouse is not at all self-centred. In such instances, compromise would become win-lose and needs to be challenged.

However, the risk that our selflessness will be exploited is far lower than we fear. This is because for most people the instinctive response to selflessness is to respond in kind rather than to take it for granted, or to take advantage of it.

By way of example, most drivers let out into busy traffic from a difficult side junction are more likely to offer a similar kindness to another driver further down the road. Conversely, if no one is prepared to let us out we are less inclined to be kind to another driver.

When we learn that we have to look out for number one because no one else will, we are more inclined to behave selfishly. When we learn that someone else is looking out for us, we are more inclined to look to the interests of another. As love begets love, so selfishness begets selfishness.

It is here that we see how important compromise is to the marriage project. Not only does compromise have a direct positive impact on the relationship, at the same time it also has a negative impact on selfishness. Compromise is the equivalent of earning double Nectar points; we build up relationship credit *and* we encourage selflessness in our beloved.

HOW TO NAVIGATE CONFLICT

Forgiveness and compromise are important ways of building up relationship credits that enable couples to build mature and trusting relationships which can withstand large goodwill withdrawals from time to time.

However, forgiveness and compromise are not a panacea for dealing with conflict. Navigating conflict certainly requires compromise and will frequently require mutual forgiveness, but conflict resolution ultimately requires honest and careful communication about the issues.

When couples are in conflict, with tempers running high, it is difficult not to be misheard. Extra care needs to be taken to try to communicate effectively. Difficult issues need to be discussed rather than avoided. Denial is not an effective long-term strategy. Following these simple dos and don'ts in communication can help couples de-escalate their conflicts.

1. *Avoid generalisations like 'you always' or 'you never'.* Such generalisations are rarely accurate. They make us feel defensive, and so we are less likely to accept the implied criticism.

2. *Speak in the first person rather than the second person.* Instead of saying 'you do this' or 'you make me feel this', try couching your concerns in terms of your own

experience and perspective. 'You're always late and that really makes me angry' is less likely to be well received than 'I feel really frustrated on those occasions when you are late'.

3. *Pick your moments.* When facing an issue that needs resolution, choosing to discuss it when either you or your spouse are already stressed, tired or busy is unlikely to lead to a constructive outcome. It is entirely reasonable to reschedule a discussion which is likely to become an argument. 'Can we talk about this after dinner or when we get in from work?' is an appropriate response as long as you do talk about it after dinner or after work.

4. *Acknowledge your own contribution to the conflict.* Conflict is rarely one-sided. If there is an issue, you are likely to have contributed to it, even if you can't quite see it. Feel free to ask your spouse their view of your contribution to the conflict if you can't see it yourself. They will certainly have a viewpoint!

5. *Allow your spouse to speak. Listen empathetically whilst they do so.* Conflict resolution is not like a debate where you listen only in order to be able to rebut their arguments. Rather, you listen in order to understand. This is more difficult for those who feel the need to win each argument. Conflict is an invitation to see the world through the eyes of another.

6. *Try to stick to the issues at hand.* Arguments between spouses can easily degenerate into a tit for tat. Rather than acknowledging that my spouse has made a valid point about my failings, it can be tempting to begin to list their failings in retaliation. This argument about money may not be the moment to point out a spouse's poor time-keeping or parenting skills.

7. *Try to remember that the way you feel now is unlikely to be the way you will feel when you are less angry.* Words cannot be unsaid. Once they have been spoken they cannot be taken back. When we are feeling our most resentful is probably not the time to make lasting decisions or to engage in constructive conflict resolution.

DISCUSSION

1. What are your reflections on the Law of Debits and Credits?

2. How difficult do you find it to create win-win compromise in your relationship?

3. Do you find it easy to forgive your partner or to seek forgiveness?

4. How have you already navigated some of the challenges of building up relationship points outlined in today's session?

5. Continue in conversation about some of the issues raised around learning to compromise and forgive after you leave. Look for opportunities for win-win compromise.

A CONCLUDING PRAYER

This or some other prayer:

Loving God, who forgives us,
even when we struggle to forgive others,
teach us to love selflessly, and to forgive.

Give us the courage
to make ourselves vulnerable in love
knowing that it is as we love others
and learn to accept love from another
that we become fully human.
Amen.

SESSION FOUR

Learn to Manage Your Finances

MANAGING YOUR FINANCES

According to the marriage charity, Relate, the number one source of arguments among married couples is to do with finances. The Money Advice Service published a report in April 2015 which indicated that 45 per cent of the couples polled lie to their partner about finances.[13] This is disturbing, though hardly surprising. Money is a significant issue in everyday life, and we hold a number of views about money that are not always rational but are usually deeply felt. Dishonesty and conflict are symptoms of a bigger set of issues around money.

As a single person, your money is your business; you are not accountable to anyone for how you spend it. If you choose to blow your salary on your stamp collection, shoe collection, handbag collection, dream holiday or season ticket, it is no one else's affair apart from your own. And if you have to live on baked beans for the next six months to be able to afford it, this is also your own concern. As a married person, however, someone else has a legitimate viewpoint on how you spend your money, and there is some level of scrutiny and accountability as well. Making that adjustment is sometimes difficult.

---

13. https://www.moneyadviceservice.org.uk/en/corporate/press-release-nearly-half-of-uk-couples-tell-money-lies-to-their-partner (accessed 20 December 2017).

However, there are additional reasons why money can be a source of conflict or dishonesty within a marriage relationship. Here are my top five:

First, money is often in short supply in the early days of marriage. Having paid for the wedding, the reception and the honeymoon, most couples start their marriages with very little money in the bank. When money is scarce, couples are more likely to argue or lie about it.

Second, when there is enough money to go around to enable both of us to do what we feel is important, money is not a problem. When there is not enough money to go around, which requires that difficult choices are made, the issues of deciding the priorities for spending and negotiating a fair sharing of resources can easily lead to discontent or dishonesty between couples.

Third, money can be a highly emotive issue and therefore a source of contention in most marriages. The issue of money is about far more than cash in the bank, or its lack; it is also an intensely personal issue which connects at the deepest levels with our sense of self-worth and well-being. Conflict about money is therefore more likely to be about a sense of well-being than disagreements about spending.

Fourth, very few couples earn similar amounts. Even when they do, child-bearing, maternity/paternity leave and childcare responsibilities often conspire to seriously undermine the earning power of one parent. For a spouse who is not earning, or is making a comparatively small financial contribution to the household coffers, the issue of money can be a difficult subject.

Fifth, among couples who either have very different attitudes towards money, or where one or both have a history of poor money management, finance will almost certainly present a problem in the relationship if it is not already doing so.

ATTITUDES TOWARDS MONEY – SAVERS VS SPENDERS

In many cases, conflicts among couples are not about money itself, but rather about conflicting attitudes towards money. Our approach to money is, like most other human activity, a learned response.

For some, money is a source of anxiety and guilt; because there never seems to be enough to go around, they feel guilty about spending it. For others, previous experience of financial hardship means they feel a need to hoard and to accumulate money to protect themselves from an uncertain future.

Yet others see money as a tool and have little interest in it, per se. They are interested in what money can do or unlock, but are less interested in accumulating it for its own sake. And, of course, there are those who are unapologetic about their wish to accumulate money – there is no intrinsic virtue in being penniless.

This range of attitudes towards money can be plotted visually on two sliding scales, one horizontal and the other vertical.

At one end of the horizontal scale are those whose default financial setting is towards saving. These are people who are always concerned about the future, and inclined towards saving for a rainy day. Their instinctive approach to money is to save for tomorrow and to invest for the future. They are not necessarily stingy or cheap, though some might be; rather, they are very careful about spending money because they know it can only be spent once. They know that spending is easier than saving so they are attentive to saving. For such people, money is important for *security*; whatever the future brings, they will be prepared.

At the other end of the scale are those who understand that money is a tool. Its purpose is to enable us to acquire goods and services that are of importance to us. Money that is not spent achieves very little. Whilst they can see the importance of saving for a rainy day, their default setting with regard to money is to use it rather than to hoard it. Such people are not necessarily wasteful of money, nor inclined to spend beyond their means; nonetheless, they see little point in scrimping today in order to save for tomorrow when the future is uncertain. The present is before us right now so their default is to spend rather than to save. For such people, money is important for *freedom*; it opens up options for them.

If the horizontal scale runs from *security* to *freedom*, the vertical scale runs from *power* to *generosity*. For those for whom money is important for *power*, they recognise that money is not only a means of acquiring goods and services; those who have money have the capacity to shape their environments, and those who don't have money work for those who do. Money is one of the ways to keep score in the game of life and they would rather have money and be a winner than not have money and be a loser. Money is the means by which our children get better education and better opportunities; it is the means by which we are able to afford to do what we would like. Money is something they need to control and which they often use to control others.

At the other end of the vertical scale are those for whom the whole point of money is to be able to be *generous*. When they don't have money it's probably because they have given it away. The primary purpose of money is to be able to do good things for the people they love. If they win the lottery, they think about buying a house for a relative who is having a hard time before thinking about spending it on a mansion for themselves. You can't take it with you so you might as well do as much good as you can with it before you go. Their aim is to finish life with very little money left in a will because they plan to give away most of it before they die.

None of these attitudes towards money are necessarily better or worse than another. They simply indicate how people think about money in very different ways, which have as much to do with our personality and psychological mind-set as with our experience and history. If both of those scales were plotted on a graph they would look something like this:

ATTITUDES TOWARDS MONEY

	Power (Controllers)	
Security		Freedom
(Savers)		(Spenders)
	Generosity (Givers)	

Exercise: Identifying yourself and identifying your partner (5–10 minutes)

In which of these four quadrants do you think your attitudes towards money are located? Which do you think best locates your partner's?

Does your partner share your views? What are the potential areas for conflict you can already identity?

SUGGESTIONS FOR MANAGING YOUR FINANCES AS A COUPLE

Setting financial goals

One of the most important things that married couples can do together is to set some financial goals. This has obvious benefits which relate to securing their financial future. However, one less obvious but equally important benefit is that setting shared financial goals enables couples who have different attitudes to money to come to an agreed mind on what they are attempting to achieve. In such cases, a husband's natural instinct to spend might be counterbalanced by his wife's inclination to save, leading to some agreed goals which are sensitive to each person's inclinations.

Setting financial goals is an important way of assessing how couples are making progress. Particularly for those who tend to be anxious about money, even when they have it, being able to progress towards goals is a critical element for their sense of well-being.

Financial goals should be time limited, specific and realistic. The best ones are reviewed annually and revised as appropriate. A financial goal might be as simple as determining how much you would like to save this year, building up a deposit for your first or next house, or planning for the dream holiday. It might be about affording university fees for your children, being able to afford to retire by fifty-five, or avoiding inheritance tax when you die. Decide what you want your money to do and then set some goals together for each year. If you set a target, you may not hit it. However, if you fail to set a target, you will be sure not to hit it!

The 20/80 rule

How much should couples be saving? There is no right answer to this, and the amount you can afford to save will change as your circumstances change. However, it is also true that if couples do not aim for some specific financial targets it is always possible to justify spending more.

One helpful guideline for couples is the 20/80 rule. Put simply, this is a target that families aim to live on 80 per cent of their household income. This is one way of understanding what it means to live within our means. Living on 80 per cent means that as household income increases or decreases, married couples adjust their living expenses. It also provides a response to the age-old question, how much is enough? Around 80 per cent.

If couples are able to live on 80 per cent, that means that 20 per cent remains. Ten per cent of household income should be saved. Depending on your attitudes towards money, these savings may provide you with a sense of security or freedom. If couples live on 80 per cent, this 10 per cent is genuinely saved, rather than put away in a savings accounts for a few weeks or months and then spent. Perhaps the best way to save is to view money saved as if it had been spent. It is therefore unavailable. At the end of the year, couples should expect their savings accounts to have grown by 10 per cent of their annual household income. For example, if your income last year was 20,000 you should expect that your savings will have increased by 10 per cent of that figure i.e. by 2,000 by the end of the year.

At various points in their lives, married couples will want or need to save more than 10 per cent. Similarly, when household income is very low or debts are very high, living on 80 per cent and saving 10 per cent will seem like a pipe dream. Nonetheless, this provides a financial goal to aspire to.

What of the remaining 10 per cent? The remaining 10 per cent is to be given away. For many who are people of faith, giving 10 per cent is part of their religious observance; it is a way of acknowledging that all that they have is a divine gift. For many who are not religious at all, giving to charity and to those less fortunate is, nonetheless, important and simply part of what it means to be a world citizen.

The wonderful thing about budgeting 10 per cent of household income to be given away is that it encourages generosity. When you are next moved by an appeal following a natural disaster and think someone ought to do something, if you have already budgeted to give away 10 per cent of your income, sending money to the Red Cross or Christian Aid is not an additional sum of money. It has already been budgeted for.

Setting a household budget and paying a fair share

Most households have less money than they would ideally like. This means that in order to set financial goals, never mind to achieve them, most households would benefit from setting a budget. A household budget is itself a short term set of financial goals. Its purpose is to help households figure out how much they want to spend, or can afford to spend, this week or month on the various areas of expenditure required for that household to run efficiently.

A good budget should include not only what you want to spend, but also what you want to save and give away. An excellent budget might start with the 20 per cent couples want to save and give away and then work on the 80 per cent available to spend. Where possible, household budgets ideally include appropriate amounts of personal cash that each spouse can spend on themselves and their interests and hobbies, safe in the knowledge that the major elements of household expenditure have already been covered.

Where both husband and wife are in employment, unless they both earn very similar amounts, this raises the question of what is a fair share of the household costs that each should bear. If one partner earns 70 per cent of the household income and the other earns 30 per cent, then that may suggest that the partner who earns more should contribute more to household expenses.

Where couples have a joint account this might be very simple. All the income goes into their joint account and all the household expenditure comes out of it. Whatever is left is shared. For those who do not have joint accounts, an alternative arrangement needs to be sought. Some couples would simply split the bills 70/30. Others couples open an account which is there only to pay bills, and each spouse pays an agreed amount into that account in order to cover all the household expenses.

For other couples it is important that there is an equal sharing in the financial responsibilities, regardless of who earns what. For some husbands in particular, it is a struggle to have a wife who earns more than they do, because their traditional understanding of the husband as provider is seriously undermined. However, there will be many wives who have similar struggles. In such cases, a fair share may be 50 per cent of the household costs because anything else would be unacceptable. Spouses such as they would feel that they are not pulling their weight.

For those who are stay-at-home mums or dads, who feel (wrongly) that they are not contributing anything to the family's financial well-being, it is important that the spouse who is earning ensures that the one who is not is not made to feel that they have no rights to household income. Part of the budgeting process needs to address the question of providing an income for that stay-at-home parent.

Couples who take the time to make and stick to a household budget and to address the question of paying a fair share can helpfully attend to a great deal of the money-related tensions from their marriage relationship.

Attitudes towards debt

In the same way that there is a range of attitudes towards money, there is a similar range of attitudes towards debt. British society as a whole is addicted to debt. Recent figures indicate that collectively we owed £239 billion in unsecured debt in 2014. This means that on average UK families each had around £9,000 of unsecured debt. This was expected to rise to £10K by the end of 2016.[14] In fact, it rose to

---

14. http://www.theguardian.com/money/2015/mar/23/average-uk-household-owe-10000-debt-by-end-2016 (accessed 21 December 2017).

just under £13,000.[15] The sharp rise is inflated by rising student debt. Without student debt the average household's unsecured debt was estimated at £7,311 in March 2017.[16] These figures suggest that conversations about attitudes towards debt will be important in most families.

Some people are simply debt-averse. They are uncomfortable with the fact that they owe someone, even if they are more than capable of meeting their monthly payments. Some extremely debt-averse people have been known to have restless nights worrying about not only their own debts but other people's as well!

Others are much more relaxed about debt. They understand that debt is a tool, like money, which allows us to achieve our ends. Even when they have money sitting in the bank, they sometimes prefer to borrow, particularly if it is a risky venture, because it is the bank's money that will be put at risk rather than their own.

Married couples need to have an open discussion about attitudes towards debt, and come to an agreed approach. This is important when the debts are well managed but even more important in instances where this is not the case, not least because a spouse who falls deeply into debt will have an impact on the other. Bailiffs at the door will not be particularly concerned to know which spouse is in debt. Though less dramatic, it is likely that poor credit ratings for one partner will mean that joint applications for mortgages or other necessary credit will be less favourably viewed. There is significant potential for conflict if, for example, couples are unable to get a mortgage because one of them has significant undisclosed credit card debts.

---

15. http://www.bbc.co.uk/news/business-38534238 (accessed 21 December 2017).
16. http://themoneycharity.org.uk/money-statistics/ (accessed 21 December 2017).

Bank accounts

Where married couples keep their money is also an area for conversation. Many married couples are committed to the idea of being one, and so keep only joint accounts. This means that all their money is jointly held, as are their debts and liabilities. Others couples maintain separate bank accounts and take responsibility for different financial obligations. So one person might pay the mortgage, another the utilities, etc.

There is, of course, no single right way to approach this issue. The key question is how couples find a way to think about their household income not as 'your money' or 'my money' but as 'our money'. This can be harder to achieve than one might think, given differing attitudes towards money.

Many married couples find a compromise solution works best, where couples maintain joint accounts for shared responsibilities but also maintain individual accounts where personal cash can be stored. If all your accounts are joint, how do you buy an anniversary present without it becoming obvious to your spouse how much was spent?

Some couples who have issues of trust may find joint accounts very uncomfortable. Couples with very differing attitudes towards money might similarly struggle. The key issue is to find a mechanism that works and is life-giving. If the current banking arrangements are a source of stress and conflict, then they perhaps should be changed.

The key issue is not what type of bank account couples keep their money in; rather, it is how couples come to see their shared income as genuinely shared. Whilst it is important to view household income as 'our money', it is also important that each spouse has at least a small amount of money that is solely theirs, for which they are not accountable and which they can spend on themselves or whatever their hobbies happen to be. What that amount is ought to be subject to negotiation.

Who takes the lead? Who keeps you accountable?

Managing money takes quite a bit of effort and intent. It should ideally be a joint effort between married couples. However, it is often the case that one person is better at, or less bored by, money management. It is probably a good idea if that person takes the lead in this area. This is not to suggest that the other partner can abdicate all responsibility for finance to their spouse. No one enjoys being the killjoy who always says, 'But we can't afford it.' So, whilst one person takes the financial lead, files bank statements, looks for the best deal on ISAs and mortgages, makes sure tax returns are completed on time, and draws up the family budget, the other needs to be part of the conversation. This shared involvement is likely to prove especially important in cases where the spouse who takes the lead in financial management earns less or is a stay-at-home parent. It would be very easy for the spouse who is earning the larger portion of the household income to feel resentment if their stay-at-home spouse tells them what they can't afford.

Importantly, someone needs to be responsible for holding the family accountable to its agreed financial goals. If your agreed goal is to clear your credit card debts in four years, then someone needs to be holding you to that goal. If your long-term aim is to raise enough money to have an adequate house for retirement, someone needs to be taking responsibility for looking at progress towards that financial goal which may be decades away.

Learning to manage your finances as a married couple can take time, even among those who have previously managed their finances well, or indeed have been in a previous relationship where financial management worked well. Making the adjustments required as a married couple will require patience, forgiveness and understanding. However, the rewards for doing so are great. In addition to whatever benefits accrue from good financial management, being attentive to this issue and being open and honest about attitudes and fears about money is an important factor in building a strong and resilient relationship. Money is not peripheral to marriage; it is in many ways central to it.

DISCUSSION

1. What are your thoughts on learning to manage your finances?

2. What are the areas that you can already identify as potentially difficult points of conflict?

3. Which of you is likely to be the person best suited to lead on finance issues?

4. Have you taken time to talk (rather than argue) about money and financial goals? If not, why not?

5. Continue in conversation around some of the issues raised around learning to manage your finances after you leave. If you have not yet had an open conversation about attitudes to money, please do so.

A CONCLUDING PRAYER

This or some other prayer:

Generous God, from whom all things come,
thank you for all that we have.
With regard to money,
teach us to be disciplined,
give us courage to be fully honest,
enable us to be generous,
empower us to be forgiving,
and free us from the temptation
to 'keep up with the Kardashians'.
Amen.

SESSION FIVE

Learn to Love and Communicate

LEARNING TO LOVE

Marriage relationships provide both opportunity and the challenge to grow in love. The challenge of growing in love is not to be underestimated. Love is, of course, an over-utilised word. We use it to describe the way we feel about a cup of tea, our favourite television programme, and we use it in the wedding vows.

So, when we say 'I love', which love exactly do we mean? Love can helpfully be categorised in three ways: Love if, Love because and Love despite.

Love if...

Love if is conditional love. If these conditions are met, then I will love. *If* you are kind to me, then I will love you. *If* you love me, I will love you. *If* you are successful, beautiful and meet my needs, then I will love you. *If* you continue to be the world-class person that you are, then I will love in response. *If* you forgive me, I will love. *If* you stop hurting me, I will love.

Most relationships are to a certain extent based on conditional love, and in many cases this is the way that relationships begin. The relationship some people have with their football teams is stereotypically conditional. If you win, we love you; if you don't, we won't. However, it does not take much to see that conditional love, a *Love if*, is not the basis upon which to build a lasting relationship.

Love because …

Love because is different to *Love if*. *Love because* does not set out any conditions but loves people the way they are, because of who they are. *Because* you are kind, *because* you are beautiful, *because* you are generous, *because* you are forgiving and gentle, *because* you are vulnerable, etc. I love you. *Because* you are who you are, I love you.

This is the kind of love often celebrated in pop music and film. I would be surprised if most relationships did not begin with some version of *Love because*. *Because* they're the kind of people they are, we love them. This is the most natural thing in the world. We are attracted to certain types of people *because* of who they are.

However, on closer examination the differences between *Love if* and *Love because* may not be as great as they first appear. If I love *because* you are beautiful or vulnerable, what happens if you are no longer beautiful or vulnerable? If I love *because* you are successful or exciting, what happens when your star wanes or you become a bit less exciting? Despite their apparent dissimilarity, *Love because* is also conditional, although perhaps less obviously so than *Love if*. *Love because* is in many ways wonderful because we love people as we find them. There is not a great deal wrong with *Love because*. Nonetheless, it is insufficient. For lasting and strong relationships, we need to move beyond *Love because*.

Love despite ...

Love despite, in sharp contrast to *Love because* and *Love if,* is an unconditional love. Rather than loving in response to good and attractive qualities, *Love despite* offers love in the face of unattractive qualities. *Despite* your flaws I love, *despite* your betrayal I love, *despite* your ugliness I love, *despite* your petty jealousy I love, *despite* the fact that I am very angry with you right now I love, *despite* legitimate reasons not to love, I love anyway. That is the challenge of marriage, to move beyond *Love if,* and *Love because,* towards *Love despite.*

Love despite, unconditional love, is the love that parents have for an unborn child. No parent says, 'If my unborn child is beautiful, well behaved and healthy then I will love them, but if they aren't I won't.' Parents take one look at their newly born child and love them, despite sleepless nights, snotty noses and nappy changes. The child does not need to do anything to earn or deserve love; we love them unconditionally, even when they drive us to the brink of exhaustion. This is also the love we discover in God, who loves unconditionally, whether we are good or bad, religious or agnostic or atheist, Christian, Buddhist, Muslim or Hindu.

This unconditional love is the basis of marriage vows – 'for better for worse, for richer for poorer, in sickness and in health'. Most married couples spend their marriage learning what it means to *Love despite.* Love is not just an emotion, but a choice – in many cases, a daily choice – to love. It is to act in love, sometimes despite our emotions.

Love is a risk

Love despite is not without risk. Offering unconditional love is to run the risk of loving those who will not reciprocate such love. It is often the unspoken fear. This fear can be especially strong among those for whom this is not their first marriage, and where some of the wounds from the previous relationship are still being carried.

If I love without reservation, might I not be taken advantage of, or taken for granted? If I love even when I have legitimate reasons not to love, do I not open myself to abuse? The short answer is 'yes'.

Unconditional love is always open to abuse. Love always makes the lover vulnerable to the beloved. To love unconditionally is no guarantee of having our love reciprocated. These risks are unavoidable when we love unconditionally. It is part of the reason that we are inclined to offer conditional love, as a form of self-defence: if you don't keep your side of the bargain, I won't keep mine.

However, nothing lasting or worthwhile is achieved without risk. If everyone sought to avoid risk, humans would never have crossed the Atlantic, climbed Everest, developed air travel or put a man on the moon. Taking risks is part of what it means to be fully alive. Moreover, anyone not prepared to take a risk of love with their spouse perhaps needs to reflect on why they are marrying them!

Nonetheless, the risk of love may not be as great as it first appears. Love has great transformative power. It is true that love always makes the lover vulnerable to the beloved. However, it is also true that love has a powerful effect upon the one who is loved.

> Monroe adopted a dog that had been rescued from an abusive situation. When she came to him, Bindy was particularly afraid of male voices, and loud noises sometimes made her incontinent. She was a cowering figure in the corner, constantly

afraid. Bindy would sometimes growl aggressively if she felt threatened, often simply by the presence of men in the room.

Monroe was patient and simply loved his new dog. She was his constant companion, at home and at work. He was patient with her paranoia and incontinence. Within three months Bindy was less often to be found cowering in a corner, within six her incontinence was cured, and within a year she was virtually unrecognisable. Her coat glowed, she was happy to bound up to strangers and her *joie de vivre* was infectious. This abused animal had been transformed by love. Never underestimate the power of unconditional love.

THE LANGUAGES OF LOVE

Having begun to learn to *Love despite*, we then need to ask, 'How is such unconditional love to be expressed?' What one person thinks is a loving action is sometimes not interpreted as such by another. One common mistake is to treat our spouse in the way we would like to be treated. After all, isn't that the golden rule?

Whilst the sentiments may be good, owing to the fact people are different – and husbands and wives, in particular – this may not work out in practice. Many wives might consider being sent for a day at a spa as a loving act. For many husbands, it would be an act of cruelty to be expected to spend a day in such a place.

Gary Chapman, in his helpful little book, *The 5 Love Languages*, argues that there are five primary ways of expressing love:

1. Words of Affirmation
2. Acts of Service
3. Receiving Gifts
4. Quality Time
5. Physical Touch.[17]

Chapman argues further that most people have a primary way of expressing love and of seeking to have love expressed to them. For a free online quiz to explore your primary love languages, see http://www.5lovelanguages.com/.

It is commonly the case that couples do not speak the same love language. It means that couples need to learn to be bilingual to express love in a language or a currency that is understood and valued.

> After spending three weeks in the Caribbean, Tim returned to the UK reluctantly. His heart was still 3,000 miles away in the islands. A few days after his return he attempted to buy something when the young woman serving him politely but suspiciously rejected the £5 note he offered her.
>
> It turned out Tim had not in fact offered her £5. Instead, he had offered her $5. An Eastern Caribbean $5 bill is small and green and after three weeks of using this currency it looked normal. Indeed, to his eyes it looked like a £5 note. However, from her perspective this EC$5 might as well have been Monopoly money. It had no value and she had no idea what it was.

---

17. For more on this, cf. Gary Chapman, *The 5 Love Languages*, Chicago, IL: Northfield, 2010.

From his perspective after three weeks in the Caribbean, Tim knew its value; it was worth roughly £1.25, more than the value of the item he was attempting to purchase. Initially, both people felt slightly offended; she because Tim was trying to palm off some dodgy cash, and Tim because his perfectly good money was summarily rejected. It was only once Tim recognised and explained the mix-up that they could laugh at the situation.

Love languages are a bit like this. One person may well be expressing love in the equivalent of Eastern Caribbean dollars, and the currency makes perfect sense to them. They know its value. However, if the object of their love is working with an entirely different currency, say pounds sterling, the expressions of love might as well be in Monopoly money. This is not only futile, it may also cause offence. However, once it is possible to recognise that love is being expressed using different love languages, it might just be possible to laugh at the situation.

Love languages are significant because they contribute to the way in which we feel in a relationship. They are the means by which we assess whether we feel loved. If your primary love language is quality time and you are married to someone whose role or personality means that they are time poor, then though showered with words of love and affirmation, or offered gifts or acts of kindness, you may nonetheless feel unloved, or at best not loved in the way you long to be.

Recognising my love language will not change the way I feel, but may enable me to see that my spouse is expressing love in a language that is not my native tongue. Similarly, it may help my spouse to attempt to change their approach.

Alternatively, love languages may help us work out why we feel under-appreciated. You shower your spouse with words of love and affirmation, buy gifts, serve them as best you know how and your spouse seems underwhelmed. Your spouse may not be an ingrate. They may just not speak the same love language.

Recognising the difference in love languages is only a first step. Trying to become bilingual is the next step and it is very difficult for some, perhaps more difficult than learning Russian or Mandarin if you are a native English speaker. In many parts of the world, people are naturally bilingual or trilingual. In a successful marriage, the challenge is to learn how to speak the love language of the other.

LEARN TO COMMUNICATE

Learning the love language of your spouse is part of a wider challenge, that of learning to communicate. Communication is key to any group or communal exercise. Communication is the lifeblood of successful relationships. Most people can think of former friends who are no longer their friends simply because they lost touch. They didn't fall out with them or stop loving them. They simply stopped communicating and the relationship died from neglect.

If the marriage relationship is not only to survive but also to grow and to flourish, couples need to develop effective ways of communicating. Communication sounds like a simple thing. And in some ways it is. In many other ways, however, communication is much more difficult than it appears because we struggle to express what we mean and to interpret what we hear. That you have ears does not make you a good listener. Communication is a skill all of us need to develop, particularly in our most important relationships.

Rob Flood, in a helpful article on familylife.com, offers five principles for communication.[18]

1. The Principle of First Response: *The course of a conflict is not determined by the person who initiates, but by the person who responds.*

In a difficult conversation it is easy to move from communication to conflict. The one who responds has the option of escalating or diffusing potential conflict.

2. The Principle of Physical Touch: *It is difficult to sin against someone while you are tenderly touching him or her.*

Touch is a significant means of communicating, and of setting a framework for communication. Couples are less like to touch during an argument. Experiment with using touch as a means of putting your words and meaning into proper context.

3. The Principle of Proper Timing: *The success of a conversation can be maximized if the timing of the conversation is carefully chosen.*

Choose your moments for communication. Your spouse may be happy to talk to you if you weren't trying to initiate conversation whilst they are in the middle of a very stressful situation, or conversely in the middle of their favourite television programme.

---

18. The bold headings below are from the website, while the text below is my summary of his comments. For more on this, cf. http://www.familylife.com/articles/topics/marriage/staying-married/communication/5-communication-tools-that-saved-my-marriage (accessed 21 December 2017).

4. The Principle of Mirroring: *Understanding can be enhanced if we measure it often throughout a conversation.*

Communication is not communication unless the other party has got the message. Until then it is meaningless babble. Those who wish to communicate well will mirror back to check to make sure they have understood. Miscommunication happens when what is said is misheard or misinterpreted.

5. The Principle of Prayer: *Success in communication is more likely when we invite God to be an active participant and guide.*

Prayer is not just for the religious. Prayer is to recognise that there is a spiritual dimension to life and relationship. Prayer is an attempt to ensure that communication is as effective as possible. When attempting to have a difficult conversation with your spouse, it can't hurt to pray about the conversation before you have it. Rather more positively, prayer is an opportunity to examine our own motives, to acknowledge our own limitations, and to seek divine wisdom.

DISCUSSION

1. What are your thoughts on learning to love, your love languages and learning to communicate?

2. What are the areas that you can already identify as potentially difficult points in your marriage?

3. *Love despite* is a description of unconditional love. How much of a challenge is it for you to love unconditionally in your relationship?

4. Talking and communication have been recurring themes in this session. How easy or difficult is for you to talk about your inner feelings as a couple?
5. Continue in conversation about some of the issues raised in this session after you leave.

A CONCLUDING PRAYER

This or some other prayer:

Gracious God,
thank you for your love for us:
deep, passionate, selfless and unconditional.
Thank you for the gift of relationship,
those whose lives enrich our own,
whose presence and love enable us
more fully to be human and more truly to be ourselves.
Fill our hearts and lives with your love
that we may offer to those you have given us
that same deep, passionate, selfless and unconditional love
which you give us so freely in your Son,
in whose name we pray.
Amen.

SESSION SIX

Learn to Express Your Sexuality

SEX CAN BE COMPLEX

Sex is an important part of the marriage relationship. It is hinted at in both the marriage vows and other parts of the marriage service. The traditional phrase 'To have and to hold' I suggest includes a sexual allusion which becomes more explicit in the words said at the exchange of rings: 'With my body I honour you, all that I am I give to you . . .'[19] Most marriage services allude to bodily union, and one form of modern Anglican liturgy prefers to speak of 'sexual union' rather than bodily union.[20]

Within Christian marriage, sex has particular importance because Christians have long argued that marriage is the proper context within which sex should be expressed: in the exclusive and lifelong relationship between husband and wife. The theory about sex is wonderful, but the reality is often much more complicated.

Unrealistic expectations

One of the complicating issues that married couples face with regard to sex is a range of unrealistic expectations. Sex

---

19. cf. http://www.i-do.com.au/wedding-tips/planning-ceremony/church-of-england-wedding-ceremony/461/ (accessed 21 December 2017).
20. cf. Common Worship, https://www.churchofengland.org/prayer-and-worship/worship-texts-and-resources/common-worship/marriage (accessed 21 December 2017).

and sexuality is a major part of contemporary human life. Films, books, music videos and adverts make a big deal of sex, and we are all supposed to have been sexually liberated in the 1960s. One of the best-selling books of 2013–14 was E.L. James's *Fifty Shades of Grey*, which many critics agree is a pretty bland book. A quick Google search will turn up any number of negative reviews. It has succeeded and has produced a film primarily because its subject matter is sex. Sex sells, but often it is someone's fantasy of sex that sells because it is so much more exciting than the real thing. Unfortunately, our overexposure to fantasy sex can build up unrealistic expectations about real sex.

The one thing that sex and prayer have in common is that people claim to be doing it more than they are in reality. Married couples need to find a sexual rhythm that works for them rather than trying to emulate what their friends appear or claim to be doing, or what public opinion appears to suggest is 'normal'.

Different expectations

Perhaps just as significant a complicating factor as unrealistic expectations is the issue of different expectations about sex. Married couples rarely have the same expectations about sex, whether this is to do with its frequency, what is permissible in the bedroom, who should initiate sex, or about its importance in their relationship.

Some of these differences are to do with the fact that people are individuals, some to do with biological differences between women and men, some with our understanding of gender and spouse roles, and many to do with prior sexual experiences, negative or positive. For many husbands, sex can be simply a physical act, divorced from intimacy. For many wives, sex needs to be an outworking of intimacy or else it is meaningless, or worse, coercive. So, a husband might be very happy to have sex with a wife whom he has ignored all day. Many wives would be less likely to be open to that idea.

All too often differences of expectation are not talked about, and may not even be fully recognised or acknowledged. Married couples need to find ways of talking about and working through their differences of expectation about sex.

Vulnerability

One of the trickiest complicating factors and perhaps the primary reason that couples find it difficult to talk about sex is the fact that sex can so easily expose our vulnerabilities. Sex is an act of intimacy in which we are literally exposed. When we are naked, there is very little of ourselves we can hide. Moreover, our sexuality is hardwired to our self-esteem. This means that when we are sexually fulfilled we feel good about ourselves, but equally when we are sexually frustrated, unfulfilled, or feel rejected or used, we feel bad about ourselves.

Put simply, negative feelings about sex are often difficult to separate from negative feelings about ourselves. A wife whose husband appears to want to have sex with her only occasionally might easily conclude it is because she is unattractive and not worth his attention. A husband who feels he is pestered by his wife to have sex could easily fear that he is not enough of a man to satisfy her needs. So, our sexuality needs to be handled with care.

Dysfunction

One significant area that contributes to married couples feeling vulnerable as far as sex is concerned is to do with sexual dysfunction. Dysfunction describes any number of circumstances that conspire to prevent married couples being satisfied in their sexual activity.

Causes of dysfunction might by physical or psychological. Physical causes include hormonal imbalances, pregnancy or childbirth, heart disease or diabetes, the side effects of medication, or simply fatigue, all of which can undermine sexual desire or performance. Psychological causes include relationship problems, stress, guilt, depression, anxiety about sexual performance, or the effects of past sexual trauma or pornography.

The Sexual Advice Association estimates that up to half of women experience some form of sexual dysfunction at some stage in their lives,[21] and up to 40 per cent of men.[22] If these statistics are accurate, most couples will experience some form of sexual dysfunction at some point in their relationship and for some couples, sex will be an ongoing challenge. The myth that needs to be exposed is the idea that everyone else is having lots of sex so there must be something wrong with *me*, if we're not.

For some couples, the issues faced may be sufficiently significant that it may be important to talk to a GP, or to see a sex counsellor or therapist. This is not something to be ashamed of; all of us need some help from time to time. There is a wealth of information available in self-help books or online, such as the Sexual Advice Association, see www.sda.uk.net.

---

21. For more on this, see http://www.sda.uk.net/wsp (accessed 21 December 2017).
22. cf. http://www.sda.uk.net/ejaculation (accessed 21 December 2017).

SEX: COMPLEX BUT IMPORTANT

So, sex can be complicated. However, precisely because of its complexity, sex is also very important, both for individual self-esteem and the health of the marriage. Sex is a medium by which couples can express love in ways that are beyond words. It is an opportunity for intimacy that is exclusive to the marriage relationship. Moreover, the vulnerability to which couples are exposed in sex is also a means of deepening their relationship. The people to whom we make ourselves vulnerable are the people we love most deeply and the people we invite to love us in return. In addition to all of this, sex can be important to our physical and mental well-being.

Though sex is important, a healthy sexual relationship does not come naturally to many married couples. Nonetheless, because sex is important, couples need to be attentive to their own sexual needs and that of their partners.

The following six points are suggestions for building healthy sexual relationships. These are not a shortcut to great sex. Rather, they are basics that should not be ignored.

1. Your most important sexual organ

Sex is a physical act; however, the most important sexual organ is the mind. In some ways this is obvious; our brain controls our sexual responses and is the location of our sexual desires and fantasies. However, the mind is more than the brain: it is also where our conscious selves reside, as well as our attitudes and fears.

The best sexual experiences, therefore, occur not when couples are merely physically stimulated, but rather when their emotions, desires and thoughts are similarly stimulated.

What happens outside the bedroom is as important as what happens inside it for healthy sexual relationships in marriage. Wives who feel taken for granted by their husbands are less likely to be able to be giving in the bedroom. Husbands who feel unappreciated by their wives sometimes lack confidence to initiate sex.

2. Practise the art of seduction

One of the challenges of marriage is that it is very easy to fall into a routine. Routines can be important but they can also become dull. In new relationships, when everything is fresh and exciting, even the thought of sex can be similarly exciting. In long-term marriage relationships, where couples know what to expect, sex can easily become perfunctory, a responsibility rather than pleasure.

Couples who want to have healthy sex in their marriage need to practise the art of seduction. For some, this comes naturally. For others, this is a really difficult discipline. Seduction is not something only husbands do for wives, or only wives for husbands. Rather, mutual seduction is to be encouraged.

Seduction is simply a way of thinking through ahead of time, 'What do I say or do to encourage my spouse to look forward to being sexually intimate with me?' Seduction might be as simple as telling your spouse how attractive they are to you, or finding ways to touch throughout the day. Alternatively, it might involve love notes, chocolate and a single rose. It will vary from couple to couple and occasion to occasion. Seduction is an art not a science, and most couples need to learn the art.

3. How much and how often?

The question of how much and how often is an area of difficulty for many couples, since it is rare that couples have the same sex drive. Depending on a variety of factors including age, energy levels, menstrual cycle, pregnancy, and physical and mental health, couples often have differing levels of sexual desire.

If a husband desires sex but his wife does not, this can cause the husband to feel rejected and the wife to feel guilty. If this is a one-off event it is unlikely to be hugely problematic. If it becomes a recurring pattern, it can very easily cause mutual resentment. There is some evidence to suggest that men typically desire sex more frequently than women, and this can be challenging to negotiate in a marriage.[23]

Couples can also measure themselves unhelpfully against others who appear or claim to be having much more sex, whether determined by regularity or duration. No two relationships are the same, however. Therefore, there is little value in making comparisons with other couples. What is much more important is to figure out what seems to be the right approach for the individual couple to the question of how much and how often. There is no single correct answer and it will vary as the relationship changes. Couples need to talk about this.

4. What is off limits?

Married couples also need to talk about appropriate levels of 'kinkiness'. Sex between married couples who have

---

23. For a recent discussion of this issue see the article by Kristen P. Mark and Sarah H Murray, 'Gender Differences in Desire Discrepancy as a Predictor of Sexual and Relationship Satisfaction in a College Sample of Heterosexual Romantic Relationships', *Journal of Sex & Marital Therapy*, Vol. 38, No. 2, March 2012, 198–215.

promised themselves to each other for the rest of their lives is a profound act of commitment and love. Married couples wanting to experiment with various ways of expressing sexual love are to be encouraged. However, if such variety causes either party to feel coerced, used or manipulated, then this undermines a healthy sexual relationship.

If certain sexual acts are considered off limits by one spouse but perhaps not the other, married couples need to talk about these openly and find a constructive way forward. Some issues are more critical and emotive than others.

On the one hand, if one spouse is keen to engage in oral sex, for example, and the other is not, this needs a conversation, perhaps several. On the other hand, despite the fact that increasing numbers of heterosexual couples are reportedly engaging in anal sex, this may be completely off limits and no serious discussion needed.[24] 'Hell no!' might be all the conversation that's required!

5. The best sex is selfless

Sex is an incredibly intimate connection when it is between two people who love and are committed to each other. At its best, sex can be a physical and spiritual expression of love, trust and intimacy that is beyond words. However, at its worst, sex can be exploitative and selfish. Even married couples are not immune from the dangers of exploitative sex.

The best sexual relationships are selfless, where ideally each seeks to give to, rather than take from, the other and

---

24. For more on this, see Aleksandar Štulhofer and Dea Ajduković, 'Should We Take Anodyspareunia Seriously? A Descriptive Analysis of Pain During Receptive Anal Intercourse in Young Heterosexual Women', *Journal of Sex & Marital Therapy*, Vol. 37, No. 5, September 2011, 346–358.

to serve the other, rather than to satisfy oneself. It might mean that sometimes a husband is happy simply to cuddle and to caress his wife because that is what his wife desires, even if he would have liked more; on other occasions, it might mean that the wife will be a little more adventurous than she is naturally inclined to be, because that is what her husband desires. It may also be the other way around, of course. If husbands learn to be selfless, wives are more likely to become selfless themselves and vice versa. However, if one person is selfish, then it is more difficult for their spouse to remain selfless.

6. Loving couples need to ***k

Think of a four-letter word ending in 'k' that means intercourse and which is crucial to marriage. The word you should be thinking about is *talk*. Not the other one.

It should be obvious by now that talking is crucial to intimacy and to mutual understanding. It is also critical to healthy sexual relationships. However, most couples find it incredibly difficult to talk about sex, whether it is to describe their difficulties or dislikes or to express their desires, what they want, what they *really* want. For many couples, it's easier to talk about sex with friends than it is with their spouse. Nonetheless, it is important that couples find ways to talk about sex sensitively, honestly, and periodically. Sexual intimacy must not be ignored. The exercise below provides an opportunity for couples to talk about sex.[25]

---

25. I'm grateful to my colleague Dr Joss Bryan for permission to use this exercise, which she developed.

Exercise: Sex Talk

Try telling your partner whether or not you think each statement is justified, and why.

Jeff has told Liz:	Liz has told Jeff:
Just because I still like looking at girlie magazines, it doesn't mean I don't love you.	It bothers me that other pretty girls can still get you going. Can't you realise you're married to me now?
It would turn me on a lot better if you wore more sexy underwear.	Why can't we just kiss and cuddle sometimes? Why do you always have to go all the way?
I wish you wouldn't always expect me to make the first move. Why can't you suggest having sex sometimes?	I wish you'd realise that I have to get in the mood before I'm ready to have sex.
I want to satisfy you, but I'm not sure how. Will you show me what turns you on?	When we have sex, will you sometimes tell me in words how it feels to you?
I want to tell you what I'd really like us to do when we have sex, but I'm afraid you'd either be shocked or laugh at me.	When I'm lit up after we have sex, why do you always turn over and go to sleep and leave me up in the air?

I love having sex with you and helping you enjoy it too. When I think that God made sex for us to enjoy each other like this, it changes my whole idea of God.	Sex with you makes me feel right and reminds me who I belong with. I'm beginning to see how God gave us sex to help us become one.

Perhaps you might try sometime soon to tell your partner something you think about sex but haven't got round to saying before now.

DISCUSSION

1. What are your thoughts on learning to express your sexuality?

2. What are the areas that you have already identified as pinch points in your marriage?

3. How easy is it to talk about sex with your partner? If easy, do you know why? If difficult, do you know why?

4. Talking and communication have been recurring themes in this session. How easy or difficult is it for you to talk about your inner feelings as a couple?

5. Continue in conversation about some of the issues raised in this session. In particular, continue the conversation started in the final exercise above.

A CONCLUDING PRAYER

This or some other prayer:

God of creation,
thank you that you have created us
in your image,
male and female,
with minds, and souls, and bodies.
Thank you for our sexuality
which energises us,
but which can also cause us distress.
Teach us both to love our bodies
which you have created,
and to express sexual love
selflessly rather than selfishly.
Hear our prayer in the name of Jesus Christ,
who became like us that we might become like him.
Amen.

SESSION SEVEN

Nurturing Your Spirituality

MARRIAGE IS A DIVINE IDEA

All across the world, in a range of diverse cultures and religions, we find the idea of marriage. Marriage does not operate in exactly the same way in each culture; some cultures practise arranged marriages, for example. Nonetheless, there are easily recognisable elements. Why is it that we find marriage in a wide range of different cultures, contexts and religions? I suggest that it is because marriage is not just a human idea, but a divine one.

Therefore, a Christian approach to marriage is based on the understanding that marriage is ultimately a divine idea. Moreover, Christian marriage is rooted in an understanding of humanity created in the image of God, i.e. a spiritual people. Those who wish to grow together as a couple need to attend to their spirituality, for married couples grow their own relationships most profoundly when they are also growing together in their relationship with God.

This final session explores ways in which married couples can nurture their spirituality, both individually and together.

RELYING ON THE MAKER

When we think of Christian marriage, we refer to more than the location of the wedding. It is also a way of saying that those who make their vows in church are seeking to make them before God. They are also seeking God's help to enable them to make and keep those vows.

The high ideals of marriage, captured in its breath-taking vows of commitment and faithfulness, provide a challenge for married couples. The response to this challenge can be either, positively, an experience of profound personal growth or, negatively, significant growth in selfishness.

The experience of entering the intimate and lifelong relationship of commitment that marriage entails will be for some an invitation to grow in generosity and selflessness, to learn intimacy and deep friendship, to flourish under the responsibilities of parenthood and be profoundly shaped by the love and forgiveness modelled and exchanged within a family.

For others, marriage can prove to be too costly an exercise; it demands more from them than they are able or willing to give. It requires too much sacrifice, too much forgiveness and too much compromise. So, they either leave the marriage or choose to remain in it at the cost of becoming hollowed-out shells of themselves, bitter about the fact that they feel trapped in a marriage they no longer want.

The difference between these two possibilities depends largely, of course, on the qualities and commitments of the people getting married. But it also depends on their capacity to rely upon the Maker to help them to make and keep their vows. If it is true that marriage is found across the world and across cultures because it is ultimately a divine rather than human idea, then it makes sense to seek to draw upon divine resources to help us make the marriage relationship flourish.

If your vacuum cleaner is made by Dyson, if it should develop a problem you would give Dyson a ring. They designed it, made it, and know what it needs to make it work best. If you drive a Jaguar, you probably rely on the people from Jaguar to help you maintain it and keep it running at its best. They made it and designed it, and know how to make it purr. If marriage is a divine idea, I suggest it is similarly reasonable that in seeking for marriage to work best, couples might want to rely on the one who designed it and made it to enable their marriage not merely to survive, but also to flourish. In Christian marriage our understanding is that only God makes it possible to make and keep our vows. So prayer is an essential part of the marriage service and of successful marriages too.

WHAT DOES IT MEAN TO BE SPIRITUAL?

To be spiritual is a way of acknowledging that the fullness of human life is not achieved once all our physical and material needs are met. Human beings need more than food, clothing, shelter, sex, security and friendship in order to flourish. We also need to discover ways of finding meaning, self-fulfilment and self-expression.

Singing and music, I suggest, are everyday examples of spiritual exercises and experience. Whether we sing in a church, a choir or the football terraces, singing is a way of moving beyond mere words to expressing who we are, what we feel and what we want to say. In singing we often use the words of others to say something about ourselves, the ones we love and the world in which we live. These words become our words and make an impression on our hearts.[26]

---

26. For a helpful article on singing as a spiritual discipline see Steven Guthrie, 'Love the Lord with All Your Voice: Singing is a Forgotten – but essential – Spiritual Discipline.' *Christianity*, 6 June 2013. http://www.christianitytoday.com/ct/2013/june/love-lord-with-all-your-voice.html?start=1 (accessed 21 December 2017).

Music and singing do something to us, in us and through us that defies simple logic, and is more meaningful than a mere collection of words and musical notes. There is a reason that we internalise and remember things more easily and more deeply when we sing them, because singing requires more than mental recall; it uses other faculties, including our spirituality.

Some would argue that sport can have a similar spiritual function. Sport appears to have no purpose beyond itself: it achieves no end; it accomplishes no work; it has very limited lasting value. Sport exists only as a spectacle for those who watch it and an exercise in competition for those who play it.

In many ways sport is not unlike art, created for pleasure rather than for any other purpose. Nonetheless, it is possible to argue that some of the best art seeks to express values and truths via a medium that is beyond words. Ideals and concepts such as truth and justice, darkness and light, hope and despair, love or betrayal have been the subject of art over the centuries.

Football, Formula One, golf, rugby or snooker may not to be attempts to express timeless concepts. They are sports that we play or watch for pleasure, and yet they have the capacity to do something to and for our souls.

To be spiritual is simply to begin to acknowledge that we have more complex needs than our physical and mental health. We need to attend to our spiritual well-being as well.

SPIRITUAL VS RELIGIOUS

For many people, attending to their spiritual well-being leads them to explore elements of religious faith. Those who choose to exchange marriage vows in a church rather than a registry office or other historic building, for example, have chosen to engage with a particular tradition of religious spirituality.

Spiritual, of course, does not necessarily mean religious. Many people recognise themselves as spiritual and realise that there is more to life and existence than the things we can perceive with our senses or quantify in scientific terms. They may believe in God or some other form of being beyond human capacity to describe or contain. However, they may simply not be inclined to be part of a church or synagogue, temple or mosque. Instead, they might prefer to practise meditation, to climb mountains or to walk, run or cycle as an avenue and a space within which they can attend to their spiritual needs.

Nonetheless, religious faith is one particular way of nurturing our spirituality and of providing a framework within which married couples can seek to grow and develop spiritually, both individually and together.

SPIRITUAL PRACTICES YOU MIGHT CONSIDER

For those couples who actively want to explore ways in which they can nurture their spirituality, here are seven recommendations.

1. Attend an Alpha course

An Alpha course is a ten-week course exploring Christian faith. It is set around a meal and is both teaching and discussion-based. At some point in the ten weeks there is a weekend away. There is no expectation that you will become a Christian or join a church if you attend an Alpha course, though many do. The course is an opportunity to explore Christian faith with a group and in a safe and relaxed setting.

Churches across the country run Alpha courses each year and there is likely to be one running nearby, possibly even in the church where couples will get married.

Other similar courses include Christianity Explored and Emmaus, though many local churches will offer their own introduction to Christianity programmes.

2. Try attending church
For couples who are not already regular churchgoers, taking the opportunity to attend church is a good way of exploring and nurturing spirituality. Couples may need to try a few churches until they find one in which they feel comfortable and where there are other couples of similar age and background. For some families, a church that is welcoming to children and provides for their needs will be even more important. Some might consider finding a local Messy Church. Messy Church is an act of worship designed for families with young children, usually based around a meal. Children take part in art and craft activities with their parents, eat together and participate in a short act of worship.

Messy Church does not necessarily take place on a Sunday or, indeed, in a church building, but might take place on a weekday in a location near to local schools. The *Messy Church Directory*, which provides a searchable database of locations by postcode, can be found at http://www.messychurch.org.uk/messy-churches.

3. Join a men's or women's fellowship or parent and toddler group
Many local churches run men's or women's fellowships. These fellowships are for activities such as sport, film nights,

book clubs and meals out, as well as for exploring spirituality and faith.

Parents and toddler groups cater for parents with young children who are not at work during the day. These groups primarily provide activities for children and a venue in which parents of young children can meet each other weekly. However, the best ones also provide opportunities to explore matter of spirituality and faith.

4. Try reading the Bible
Bible-reading is for many people an important way of thinking about spirituality and nurturing faith. Well-known actor David Suchet, perhaps best known for playing Agatha Christie's *Poirot*, tells the story of how he began his journey towards Christian faith when he read a Bible in his hotel room.[27]

There are many Bible-reading guides available and most smartphones and tablets can download Bible apps. Many of the better apps offer the option of reading the Bible aloud so that you can listen to it whilst doing something else. Perhaps fittingly, the New International Version has David Suchet himself reading the Bible on an eBook.

5. Acts of service
Spirituality is often nurtured through service to others, whether volunteering in your local charity shop, becoming a leader for the Boys' Brigade or Brownies, or contributing to and helping with a food bank.

Acts of service help to remind us that we are part of a bigger story and encourage us to be less self-centred and

---

27. For an account of this story, see the interview here: http://www.thestar.com/entertainment/stage/2014/04/25/david_suchet_and_the_mystery_of_faith.html (accessed 21 December 2017).

more generous, but they also have the practical benefit of helping others.

6. Mindfulness

Mindfulness has its roots in an ancient Buddhist practice. Mindfulness from a Christian perspective is about 'looking at the here and now with a sense of curiosity and wonder'. It's a decision to live in the now rather than turning over the past and worrying about the future. Being still before God and hearing him speak is something Christians have practised for centuries: 'Be still and know that I am God'.[28]

> The idea behind mindfulness is straightforward: 'paying attention on purpose, moment by moment, without judging'.[29]

'Mindfulness does not conflict with any beliefs or tradition, religious, cultural or scientific. It is . . . a practical way to notice thoughts, physical sensations, sights, sounds, smells – anything we might not normally notice.'[30]

Mindfulness is primarily a way of slowing down, of paying attention, of being reflective, taking the time to be still and to see the action of God in all that is around us. Some Christians are concerned about the Buddhist roots of mindfulness. Baptist pastor and New Wine leader, Shaun Lambert, counters this by arguing that 'claiming mindfulness is Buddhist is like claiming gravity is British because Sir Isaac Newton discovered it'.[31]

---

28. For more cf. 'The Lost Gospel of Mindfulness', *Premier Christianity* magazine, April 2015.
29. David Derbyshire, 'Should we be mindful of mindfulness?', *The Guardian*, 23 February 2014, www.theguardian.com/society/2014/feb/23/should-we-be-mindful-of-mindfulness-nhs-depression (accessed 21 December 2017).
30. http://www.getselfhelp.co.uk/mindfulness.htm (accessed 21 December 2017).
31. cf. 'The Lost Gospel of Mindfulness', *Premier Christianity* magazine, April 2015. cf. also Shaun Lambert, *A Book of Sparks: A Study in Christian Mindfulness*, Watford: Instant Apostle, 2014.

7. *Prayer*

Prayer is perhaps the most direct of spiritual disciplines; it is an attempt to speak with and hear from God.

For some, prayer is the most simple of spiritual disciplines, for to pray is to say what is on our hearts and minds; it is to bring to God, whether aloud or in silence, our concerns and our fears, our sorrows and frustrations, our joy and wonder, our confusion and our desire for a better world. Prayer can be done alone or with others, on our knees or as we walk, in private or in public, in ordered acts of worship or in the chaos of everyday life.

For others, prayer is among the most difficult of spiritual disciplines because it feels too one-sided, too inactive, too contemplative, too much like talking to ourselves. Nonetheless, prayer is worth exploring because it is not just about us talking to God, it is also about placing ourselves in a posture where God might speak to us in ways that we might not anticipate or imagine.

Nurturing your spirituality is not a way of saying 'become religious' or 'join a church'. It is a way of acknowledging that all spouses are spiritual people who will need spiritual resources if they are to navigate the challenges of marriage.

DISCUSSION

1. What are your thoughts on nurturing your spirituality?

2. Do you already have some spiritual practices? What are they, and what benefit do you derive from them?

3. Prayer can be the simplest and the most difficult of spiritual exercises. What are your thoughts on prayer? Do you pray already?

4. If you were invited to attend church as a way of being attentive to your spirituality, is that an invitation you would welcome?
5. How important is thinking about or engaging with God for your everyday life? What would help you to be more fully human?
6. Please continue in conversation about some of the issues raised in this session after you leave.

A CONCLUDING PRAYER

This or some other prayer:

God, who has created all things good,
thank you for both the challenges
and the blessings of marriage relationships.
Teach us to be selfless rather than selfish,
forgiving rather than keeping score,
faithful rather than faithless,
more inclined to give than to receive.
Transform us, we pray,
into better versions of ourselves
so that we become better reflections
of the God in whose image we were created.
May our love for each other
be infused by your immeasurable love
for us and all you have made.
Amen.